Diamonds from the KING

Lessons from an ordinary life

CHRISTINE BULLOCK

Ark House Press
arkhousepress.com

© 2022 Christine Bullock [www.bullockc.com]

All rights reserved. Apart from any fair dealing for the purpose of study, research, criticism, or review, as permitted under the Copyright Act, no part may be reproduced by any process without written permission.

All Scripture quotations, unless otherwise indicated, are taken from the Holy Bible, New International Version®, NIV®. Copyright ©1973, 1978, 1984, 2011 by Biblica, Inc.™ Used by permission of Zondervan. All rights reserved worldwide. www.zondervan.comThe "NIV" and "New International Version" are trademarks registered in the United States Patent and Trademark Office by Biblica, Inc.™

Some names and identifying details have been changed to protect the privacy of individuals.

Cataloguing in Publication Data:
Title: Diamonds From The King
ISBN: 978-0-6453714-6-8 (pbk)
Other Authors/Contributors: Bullock, Christine;

Design by initiateagency.com

Contents

Foreword vii
Preface ix
Introduction xiii

Diamonds of Identity

Section 1: Who am I? 3
    Chapter 1: A Lifelong Journey 5
    Chapter 2: Liked by God 10
    Chapter 3: Good Girl 17
    Chapter 4: Growth 22

Section 2: What am I? 29
    Chapter 5: Matter Matters! 31
    Chapter 6: Glory 38
    Chapter 7: Light 43
    Chapter 8: The Treasure and the Merchant 48
    Chapter 9: The Image of the Lord 55

Diamonds From Experience

- Section 3: Where's God When Life Hurts?..................................67
  - Chapter 10: Overlooked..69
  - Chapter 11: Mum 74
  - Chapter 12: Grief...84
  - Chapter 13: What a Year...90
  - Chapter 14: Cancer?...95
  - Chapter 15: Strength in Weakness 104
- Section 4: When God Does the Unexpected 109
  - Chapter 16: An Encounter with Holy Spirit.............................111
  - Chapter 17: Disappointment 118
  - Chapter 18: The Potter 125
  - Chapter 19: Most Highly Favoured Lady 130
- Section 5: God in the Everyday 137
  - Chapter 20: Friends with God?..139
  - Chapter 21: The Radiance of God's Glory 146
  - Chapter 22: Fear 152
  - Chapter 23: Leaving and Cleaving 157
  - Chapter 24: Love the One You're With 162
- Conclusion 167
- Endnote 171
- Group Discussion Questions 175

This book is dedicated to all the people at Riverlife Baptist Church who have journeyed with me in good times and bad, who have prayed and laughed and taught me, who have taken risks with God, and opened their hearts to share what they have learnt. Thank you.

It is also dedicated to Pastor Pat Hegarty. He was the one who first taught me that Spirit and Truth were not in conflict, that I could open myself to the Holy Spirit without abandoning my mind. His wisdom and keen intellect combined with his passion for God and openness to the things of the Spirit were transformational for me. Thank you, Pat.

Foreword

One thing that I have learnt over my twenty-three years of pastoral ministry is that everyone has a life story worth telling and we can all learn something from other people's stories. Christine's story is one we can all relate to. She, like many of us, has had her fair share of ups and downs, but what has impacted me is how she has been able to identify how God's grace has brought about transformation to her life. Christine would describe this as, 'God taking us as graphite, and through Jesus' death changing us into diamonds'.

Diamonds from the King is more than gaining insight into the personal world of Christine Bullock. While it is a reflection on some of her life changing moments, it really does speak to all of us about key elements in our relationship with God. You will be challenged to take a closer look at your own faith, identity, trust and love as Christine unpacks her own journey with God.

I've had the privilege of knowing and working alongside Christine at Riverlife Baptist Church (formally Kenmore Baptist Church), in her roles as Elder and staff member. I can truly say that her open and honest pursuit of God's presence has allowed Him to cut many facets in her, and that she genuinely reflects the glory of God.

As a friend, I knew of some of her life story and as a pastor, I journeyed with her through some of the highs of encountering Holy Spirit and the lows of cancer diagnosis. Still, I was intrigued by Christine's candid re-telling of these events and the lessons she has learnt.

Through *Diamonds from the King*, Christine is encouraging us to take a closer look at our own life journeys and to invite God into every moment . Essential to growing in Christlikeness is how open we are to inviting King Jesus into not only the times of great joy and celebration, but also the times of grief and heartache. Christine clearly shares how even the more disappointing moments in life can lead to another way God allows His glory to be reflected through us, if we let Him.

God hasn't finished with Christine, nor has He finished with us. God is still looking to make every moment an opportunity for His faithfulness to be made evident to all.

Do yourself a favour: pick up this book and read it! In your hands you will find gems from the Lord that I am certain will bring you encouragement and stir your faith. Take a chapter at a time and reflect upon your own journey to see how God is transforming you into a precious diamond of His own.

John Robertson
Senior Pastor,
Riverlife Baptist Church,
Brisbane, Australia

Preface

I never imagined myself writing a book. I wrote in response to a strong sense of God's prompting to share some of the truths He has taught me and the blessings He has given me. The whole process has taken so much longer than I first imagined, and I felt like giving up many times, but I could never let go of the feeling that I had to do it. And now it is done! Praise God! It is only through His goodness and kindness that it has gotten this far.

God has used so many people to first produce the diamonds that I share, and then to form them into a book. I will try to thank them now.

First, my darling husband Rob. Rob has journeyed this road with me, shared my joys and my tears, my triumphs and my failures. We have wrestled with God together and rejoiced in Him together. Rob's keen spiritual awareness, love for God and piercing intelligence have been a wonderful sounding board as I have struggled to find God in the midst of disappointment and opened myself to new ways of seeing Him. Rob, you are God's greatest gift to me after Himself, and I am so grateful!

There are so many dear friends who have blessed me in countless ways. I am too scared to list them, because I am sure to overlook someone, but to all those who have supported me, prayed with me, comforted and encouraged me, shared their wisdom and their vulnerability, thank you. Each of you have left your mark on me.

I want to thank my family, both the one I grew up in and the family that God has given to Rob and me. Dad and Mary, Robert, Peter and John, it is always a delight to be together to discuss some thorny issue or to do life together. You have all helped to make me who I am, and I am grateful for each of you, and for your families. David, Jessica and Stephen, you are each a joy to me. You are wise and funny and smart and kind, and you are always there when I need you. Katie and David, our dear daughter- and son-in-law, thank you for welcoming us into your lives and becoming an integral part of the Bullock clan. And our darling grandchildren Charlie, Lachie and Isabelle (and any others God may send us), you are my joy and my delight. God bless you.

I have been part of three church communities while I was writing this book, and I want to acknowledge each of them. As mentioned in the introduction, I will always be grateful to the community of Riverlife Baptist Church. Your openness to Holy Spirit and risking new things with Him created an atmosphere where my faith journey became an adventure again. Kenmore Church of Christ, it was such a blessing to be part of your inception and have an opportunity to pass what I had learned on to others. I'm so excited to see what God is doing in you. And HumeRidge Church of Christ, we have appreciated the warm welcome we have received as we have relocated to a new city and a new community, and we're excited to see what God has in store.

Much of the writing of this book was undertaken while I was studying my Master of Divinity at Malyon Theological College. Thank you to each of the staff and students who shared their wisdom with me. The deep learning I experienced both in lectures and in discussions on campus with fellow students has, I hope, made this book more theologically rigorous, and has strengthened my walk with God.

Many of my friends read my book at various stages of its writing. Thank you to you all for your encouragement and suggestions. A particular thankyou to Rebekah Bickerton and Linda Paech who generously edited it for me. You have both improved it immensely! Also to Karen Hales who had the idea of using the characteristics of diamonds for the reflection questions at the end of each chapter.

Thank you to Pastor John Robertson for your foreword, and for all your encouragement and teaching over the years.

Thank you to the team at Ark House Press for all your work in bringing this book to its final form. You are awesome!

And finally, thank you to you, the reader. I have imagined you and prayed for you as I wrote, and now as I send my words out into the world I pray that as you read and ponder you will be blessed as I have been blessed. Please accept these stories as a gift from one pilgrim to another.

Introduction

You shall be a crown of beauty in the hand of the Lord, and a royal diadem in the hand of your God. You shall no more be termed Forsaken, and your land shall no more be termed Desolate, but you shall be called My Delight Is in Her, and your land Married; for the Lord delights in you, and your land shall be married.
—Isaiah 62:3-4 ESV

Diamonds are special. They seem timeless, unable to be corrupted or damaged. I have a beautiful diamond ring that has passed through four generations of women in my family. It is the engagement ring that my great-grandfather gave to my great-grandmother in 1906. When she died it passed to my grandmother, who gave it my mother, who left it to me. When I received it the setting was worn and fragile and the band very thin from eighty years of wear, but the diamonds were bright and clear, seemingly unaffected by the passage of time.

Diamonds are forged in pressure and heat. They must be dug from the earth then cut and polished before their beauty is fully seen. Each diamond has value, but that value is dramatically increased when it is prepared and set by the hands of a master.

Diamonds are made of carbon. But they are not the only form that carbon takes. Carbon is far more commonly found as graphite. Graphite is black and soft, soft enough to write with (its name comes from the Greek word for writing). Diamonds are clear and hard. Graphite crumbles under pressure, but diamonds are incredibly strong. Graphite is softer than most substances, whereas diamonds can cut almost anything. Graphite is a lubricant; diamonds are an abrasive. Graphite absorbs the light; cut and polished diamonds reflect and refract it, creating sparkles and rainbows. And yet, both are carbon. While their essence is the same, their nature is radically different. God takes us as graphite, and through Jesus' death changes us into diamonds. The essence of who we are remains the same, but our nature and our characteristics are radically different.

God doesn't want to destroy anything in our lives. Yes, our sinful nature must die, but it is resurrected in a new form. Satan has never created anything – he can only take the good things God made and twist them, tempting us to take them to excess or enjoy them in the wrong way or place. God gave us hunger, and desires that it be satisfied; Satan takes hunger and makes it greed. God wants us to enjoy who we are; Satan takes that and makes pride. God wants us to be interested in each other; Satan turns that into gossip.

When we bring our sins to God, rightly confessing and renouncing them, He doesn't want to cut them out of us and throw them away. He wants to restore them to what they were meant to be. God wants to take our graphite, our black, dull sinful nature, and transform it into diamonds, precious jewels that reflect His light.

We see this in the verses I quoted at the beginning of this section. They are addressed to Israel, but I believe He is also saying them to us. When it talks about the land being married it signifies a restored relationship with God, as marriage is often used as a metaphor for the relationship between God and Israel. God is transforming us into royal diadems, transforming the parts of us that were forsaken and desolate and changing them into things in which He can delight. He is working in the areas of our lives that are broken and disconnected from Him and bringing restored commitment and connection. Perhaps you might like to read these verses out loud, putting in 'I' where it says 'you', as it is here:

> *I shall be a crown of beauty in the hand of the Lord, and a royal diadem in the hand of our God. I shall no more be termed Forsaken, and our land shall no more be termed Desolate, but I shall be called My Delight Is in Her, and our land Married; for the Lord delights in me, and our land shall be married*

I am one of those privileged people who has grown up all her life knowing God, being born into a Christian family and being taught about Him since I was little. I formally "gave my life to Christ" when I was eleven, but I don't remember there ever being a time when God was not a real presence in my life, whom I loved and wanted to obey.

When I was a teenager, I was a big fan of Christian autobiographies, which were generally stories of the person's terrible life of sin before their dramatic conversion. I hated the fact that I had never rebelled and so had no such story to tell. But I have learnt that God uses each of our stories to bring glory to Himself, no matter how boring our stories seem to us. I guess that is why I am now writing this book!

Even with the privilege of a lifetime walking with God, I am still dealing with my misconceptions of who I was and who God is. All of us are broken and damaged in some way, no matter what our upbringing. Part of what I record in this book is the way that God has been constantly at work in my life unraveling the lies and healing the places that were broken and damaged.

Satan loves to take God's truths and twist them into a lie. For me, He took the truth that we are sinful and need God to redeem us and made it into a lie that I must work hard to be good enough for God to love me. Satan took the truth that as I walk with God, my behaviour will change, and made it into the lie that I must change my behaviour so that I can walk with God. Satan got my eyes off God's invitation to be in fellowship with Him and got me futilely striving to be good enough for God, making my faith into a heavy burden of religion.

You probably have different lies that you have believed about yourself and God. As you read about some of the lies I have believed, ask God to start to reveal your lies to you. Replacing lies with truths sets you free to live the way that God intends you to live! Often in order to replace the lie, we need to forgive the person or people who caused us to believe that lie in the first place, even if they never meant us any harm. Asking God the questions, 'What lie am I believing? Who do I need to forgive? What's the truth?' whenever I come to a roadblock in my life has been so helpful (I first learned to ask these questions from Bethel Sozo training).

As I journey with Jesus through my life, God takes things that seemed rubbish and transforms them. He brings blessing out of apparent disaster and changes the way I see myself and Him. *Diamonds from the King* is my story about His goodness. I pray that you see sparkles of eternal diamonds in my stories of God's faithfulness. Please keep what is helpful and forget anything that isn't!

Each chapter has a page at the end to help you to apply the content to your own life. It is in four sections named for the characteristics of diamonds: Clarity, which is a Bible verse for you to meditate on; Cut, which is a question or questions to ask of God to reveal lies you've been believing; Colour, which is a reflection question for your journal of truths that God wants to highlight; and Carat, which is a declaration that you can speak out loud over yourself, to reinforce the truth discussed in the chapter. You might like to get a special journal to use as you journey through this book. There is also a group discussion guide at the end of the book in case you would like to work through it with some friends. Other resources may become available from time to time on my website www.bullockc.com.

I often talk about asking God questions. I find this is a very helpful way to pray. I ask Him a question and then I wait to see if I receive any impression from Him. I have never heard an audible voice, but as I pray I often find that the Holy Spirit answers my questions in subtle ways, as I take the time to listen. Of course, these impressions need to be weighed against the Bible, but Jesus promised that His sheep would hear His voice (John 10:3-4). I pray that as you read this book and reflect on it with God that He will guide you and teach you the truths that you need at this time. God bless you!

Diamonds Of Identity

Lessons from God about who I am in Him

SECTION 1

Who am I?

Chapter 1

A Lifelong Journey

A couple of years ago as I was praying, I sensed God bringing to my mind different times in my life when I chose to love Him and worship Him. It was like a series of flashbacks of me at different ages, responding whole-heartedly to God's love.

I saw myself as a little girl, sincerely praying before going to sleep: 'Dear God, please make all the bad people good, and all the good people, better.' This, while I pictured all the people in jail going to church, and all the people in church running out happy!

I saw myself as a child lying in bed offering my life to Jesus and asking Him to come and fill my heart.

I saw myself as a teenager at a church camp, sitting outside on a frosty Canberra night, looking at the stars and worshipping God, full of awe at His majesty and creativity and overwhelmed with love for Him.

I saw myself in my early twenties, kneeling and offering myself to God for Him to use however He wished, promising that no matter what it cost, I would serve Him all my life.

I saw myself as a young woman walking down the church aisle following my mother's coffin at the end of her funeral, choosing to rejoice that she was now in 'the church triumphant' even though my heart was breaking.

I saw myself in my forties lying in bed offering my body as a living sacrifice to God as I came to terms with a probable stage four cancer diagnosis, trusting Him to do with me as He willed and rejoicing in His goodness.

I saw myself faithfully choosing God, time after time throughout my life. In picture after picture I was loving God. I felt that God was telling me that that is the beautiful collage that He sees when He looks as me: a rich, multi-dimensional picture of my walk with Him, and all the ways I have chosen love and obedience.

I asked Him about all those other times, the times of fear and doubt and sin and failure. These are the episodes I tend to remember when I think of my walk with Him. But He wasn't interested in those; they had been washed away by Jesus.

For some reason, I always thought that God's main focus was on my sin. I thought that He was like that teacher who never noticed when you did something right but was on you the minute you messed up. I felt like my position as God's child was tenuous, like someone on probation. I was afraid that I had to walk on eggshells with Him and couldn't trust Him with the worst of me. I was afraid of rejection.

But it says in His word, *'Once you were alienated from God and were enemies in your minds because of your evil behaviour. But now He has reconciled you by Christ's physical body through death to present you holy in His sight, without blemish and free from accusation—if you continue in your faith, established and firm, and do not move from the hope held out in the gospel.'* (Colossians 1:21-23).

When I read this, I realised that I didn't believe it. I knew that I wasn't holy and without blemish. But I had to choose whether to accept what God says about me or to cling to my own opinion.

That day He showed me that what really catches His attention is the times we act like His kids. Not that He doesn't hate sin. He does. And not that sin doesn't matter. It matters so much that Jesus died to conquer it. But God is not focused on it. Our sins are not tattooed on us in indelible black ink, forgiven but never forgotten. Rather they are washed white as snow, and we are made new.

DIAMOND

When you have given yourself to Him God's
focus is on you, not on your sin.

Clarity
From the Word – A truth to stand on
For He chose us in Him before the creation of the world to be holy and blameless in His sight. Ephesians 1:4
Therefore as God's chosen people, holy and dearly loved, clothe yourselves with compassion, kindness, humility, gentleness and patience. Colossians 3:12

Cut
Ask God to reveal a lie you've been believing about how He sees you. Write it down. Ask God if there is anyone you need to forgive in relation to this lie, and if you can, forgive them. Now, ask God to reveal to you what His truth about this lie is and write it in your journal, so that when that lie tries to rear its head again, you can come back to it and stand on that revealed truth.

Colour
For your journal: God, as I set this time aside to just sit with You and listen, will You reveal to me some of the things You treasure about me?

Carat
Declaration: Thankyou Lord that You chose me and You created me to be loved. I am Your beloved treasure. You don't focus on my faults and failures; You look on me with love, and You see me as holy and unblemished.

Chapter 2

Liked by God

For the longest time I never really thought that God liked me. I knew that He loved me – He had to, because He is God, and God is love – but I was pretty sure that He didn't like me much. My understanding of my salvation went something like this:

Jesus died on the cross to pay the price for my sins. If I accepted Him into my heart, He took His robe of righteousness and put it on me, so that when God looked at me He didn't see me, but He saw Jesus. I then had to try really hard to make myself good enough for God to eventually be happy with me, and maybe even one day look at me. The picture I had in my head was that I was this dirty, smelly, sinner hiding in the corner of God's throne room, with Jesus' robe of righteousness covering my filth, and Jesus standing in front of me so that God didn't see any dirt that still may be showing. He pretended that I was clean, even though He could clearly see and smell my rubbish.

I saw my salvation as a lie – a polite fiction that God engaged in because of what Jesus had done – not as any real change in me. And because I didn't believe that God saw the real me, I naturally didn't feel loved by Him. He loved this pretend person that Jesus created. It was such a devilish twisting of the truth. Of course, I didn't fully realise the lie that I was believing about God and me. I just knew how unloved I felt, and how hard I had to work to try to be good enough for God.

I had been a Christian many years before God really opened my eyes to what I had been believing. I was out early one morning, walking and talking with God. And I sensed God telling me a story. Now to understand this story, you need to know that I love history. This story is set in the pioneer days of America, when it was possible to get a homestead grant of one hundred and sixty acres for free from the government, on the condition that in five years you improved the land and built a dwelling of at least twelve by fourteen feet.

This story is about a man called John. He took a homestead grant, but his problem was that he didn't have any skills or tools or materials to build a house. So, he spent his days scrabbling around in the dirt, trying to make something that would pass as a house. His father saw what was happening, so he offered to build a house for him. John accepted, and his father built him a homestead. But it wasn't just a simple dwelling that would meet the requirements of the grant. He built him a beautiful, generous home with everything he could need for gracious living. It had a gourmet kitchen, and a guest wing, and a music room and an art studio and verandas for sitting on in the cool of the evening, watching the sunset.

Now when the Lands Office official came, John could stand at the door of his house and proudly proclaim, 'The requirements of the law have been met. The land belongs to me and my descendants forever.' But John didn't believe in his heart that the land was properly his. He hadn't earned it. He hadn't built the house. So, he never lived in the house. He didn't cook in the kitchen or paint in the art studio. He didn't crop the land or do anything to benefit from the house and land he had been given. And the people who should have been blessed from his abundance missed out. He didn't host amazing parties or give hospitality to the needy. His farm didn't contribute to the local economy. Instead, he spent the rest of his life trying to build a house from whatever rubbish he could find, in order to prove that the land was truly his.

This story cut me to the core. I could see how my understanding of my salvation as a legal fiction, where God pretended I was OK so that I could go to heaven, stopped me from having a real relationship with Him. I still thought it was my job to fix myself, to build my own righteousness. And I saw how in doing that I was rejecting the abundant life that Jesus was offering me. John chose to spend his life in the dirt trying to achieve something that was impossible for him, while refusing to use what the father had given him to do the work he was made to do. In doing so, he was not being noble or self-denying; he was just being stupid and pig-headed. It was the same with me. Jesus offered me abundant life and complete righteousness as a free gift, but I refused to live from that, and instead stubbornly tried to build my own righteousness. But it was never going to happen. The harder I tried to become righteous in my own strength, the more I was aware of my failure. I might have been able to manage my outward behaviour, but I could see that my heart was full of mixed motives. If I succeeded in being 'good' then I became proud and judgmental; if I failed, I was tempted to despair.

I had always struggled to understand how law and grace went together. I knew that salvation was a free gift of God, but there were still all those commands in the New Testament about righteous living. How does that work? This story helped me to understand that I don't have to work to build my own righteousness – that is a free gift won for me by Jesus on the cross – but I have to live in that righteousness. In my story, if John had moved into the house then it wouldn't mean that he spent the rest of his life sleeping. On the contrary, his life would have been full. He would have been cooking in the gourmet kitchen, painting in the art studio, making music in the music room and so on. What he wouldn't have been doing was trying to build a house. The moment I stop trying to build my own righteousness, I am free to stop striving to accomplish something I can never accomplish. I am free to stop living in the shame of the mess of my building attempts. I am free to live fully the life God planned for me. To create and serve and love, confident that I myself am loved and secure. There will still be times I make mistakes and times that I sin, but they are not disasters because they don't affect my basic relationship with God – they just need to be confessed and repented of so that we can move forward. I can stop living in fear of rejection and failure, because my righteousness is no longer my responsibility.

The concept of our righteousness is explained by Paul in Romans 4. He says that God credits our faith to us as righteousness. The Greek word Paul uses for 'credit', logizomai, is an accounting term. Our account is credited with righteousness, even though we have not earned it and have no right to it. But God gives it to us, and it is ours. If a billionaire gave me a credit card and told me that I now had unlimited credit and could buy whatever I liked, I would have a choice. I could choose to believe her and live my life in a new way with abundance, or I could choose to think it was too good to be true and continue living in poverty. When we choose to believe that God is telling the truth when He declared us as righteous, then we can live as righteous people. We still sin – we are still being sanctified - but we have the status of righteous people. We don't have to cringe in God's sight, waiting for His condemnation. He says in Romans 8:1 that there is no condemnation for those that are in Christ Jesus. NO CONDEMNATION. Not a little bit, not some, but no condemnation. We need to believe God when He says this and to live in this truth.

Before I understood this, my basic reaction to God was, 'I'm sorry', even if I didn't really know what for. My eyes were continually fixed on my failure. Living in righteousness means taking my eyes off myself. It means trusting that God's sight is better than my sight and releasing my need to earn His love through my own hard work. It means letting go of comparison, because I don't need to compare my rubbish heap attempt at building righteousness with anyone else's. It means being able to enjoy being the unique person that God made me to be.

Living from righteousness means living in joy. It is a change in thinking. When I was trying to build my own righteousness, I needed to be good because otherwise I would be punished. When I live in God's righteousness, I am good because that's who I am as God's child. When I was struggling to build my own righteousness I was continually trying to make myself less. I tried to suppress my desires because I assumed anything I actually wanted must be wrong. When I am living in God's righteousness I am free to explore the different aspects of the person that He has created me to be. I am able to be creative with Him, to enjoy His good creation and my brothers and sisters.

As I pursued this journey with God, I rediscovered passions I had forgotten. I began to dance, to paint, to write. Life became richer and fuller. I have so much more to offer others now. I don't have to live in fear of rejection by God, and I am free to be myself.

DIAMOND

God gives us the free gift of righteousness through Jesus Christ. That gift gives us freedom to live as we were made to live.

Clarity
From the Word – A truth to stand on
For if, by the trespass of the one man, death reigned through that one man, how much more will those who receive God's abundant provision of grace and of the gift of righteousness reign in life through the one man, Jesus Christ!
Romans 5:17

Cut
Ask God to show you some ways that you have been trying to build your own righteousness, and the impact that has had on you and your relationship with Him.

Colour
For your journal: Ask God to show you what your house of righteousness might have in it. What are some of the ways He wants you to live abundantly? What are some gifts He has given you that He wants you to develop, or some passions He is inviting you to explore?

Carat
Declaration: God has made me righteousness. I do not have to be afraid or ashamed. I can live an abundant life through faith in Jesus Christ.

Chapter 3

Good Girl

Not long after the experience described in the last chapter I thought I heard God tell me, 'I don't want you to be a good girl.' I was confused. If not a good girl, then what? A bad girl? He left me sitting with this thought for a few weeks, and I felt resentful. What was wrong with being a good girl? I had always done my best to do the right thing. I WAS a good girl. I was a good girl at school, I was a good girl at home. I never was in detention at school, I never rebelled against my parents. I got good grades, worked hard, kept the rules. As an adult I did everything that was expected of me. I went to church, I prayed, I volunteered. What was God's problem? Wasn't this how I was supposed to live?

After a few weeks, God told me a bit more. 'You don't have to be a good girl for me to love you.' He showed me the older brother in the prodigal son story (Luke 15:11-32). He was a Good Boy who did all the right things, but he didn't understand his father at all. He thought what was required of him as a son was service, and he was full of judgement of his brother. When he was confronted with his father's love for his rebellious younger brother the older brother's response was anger. From his point of view, he'd been slaving away all these years for his father, and yet he'd never even been given a goat. His understanding of their relationship was all about obedience and reward, not love and fellowship.

The parable of the Prodigal Son says so much to me about identity. I don't think either son really knew who they were. They both thought that the way to their father's heart was to serve him. When the younger son rebelled, he thought that the only way back into the family was to give up his rights as a son and become a servant. The older brother thought that he had earned rights to his father's care by serving him obediently all his life. Neither considered that what their father really wanted was sons with whom he could share his life and his dreams; sons whom he could bless and enjoy.

The problem was that neither seemed to value the father for who he was, only for what he could give them. The younger son wanted his father's money and the freedom that would bring, and then when that failed he wanted the father's resources so that he could stay alive. The older son thought that he too deserved a party, that his hard work deserved a reward. Neither realised the pain that the father felt at the loss of his younger son, or at seeing the slave-mindset of his older son.

How often do we do this to God? How often do we fall into the mindset of thinking that God wants us to serve Him because He needs serving? How ridiculous, to think that God could have a need of us! How often do we tick off our Christian duties like 'Quiet Times' and weekly church attendance, thinking that then we deserve to have God bless us? How often do we think that God is valuable because of what He can give us or what He can withhold from us, rather than because of who He is?

As I reflected, I saw that a lot of my desire to be good was born out of fear. I was too afraid to not be good. This was another fruit of my belief that I had to earn God's love, and that He didn't really love me. The lies I was believing about who I was, and who God was, kept me far from

Him. Being afraid of His displeasure meant that I didn't really want to be with Him. Being a Christian seemed like hard work, and spending time with God just made me feel guilty. Every time I sinned, I thought that I needed to pay for it in some way. I was behaving like the younger son, who thought his sin meant he could only ever be at home as a hired worker. I reasoned that if I sinned then God couldn't possibly want me as a daughter and that I would need to be a servant, at least for a while, until I had suffered enough to be allowed to enter His presence again. But the trouble was that all I saw was my sin, so I never 'deserved' to enter God's presence. And of course, none of us deserve to be with God. But He doesn't need me to earn the right to enter His presence. It is His free gift to me through Jesus Christ. And by refusing to enjoy it, I am scorning the incredible sacrifice that Jesus made on my behalf.

As a mum, I think of how I would feel if my kids apologised extensively every time they saw me. I would be concerned that there was something very wrong in our relationship. It would be so frustrating – my desire for my kids is for time with them, not for constant apologies. Of course, I want them to be sorry for things that they do wrong, but not a reflex of *'sorry, sorry, sorry'* upon seeing me. But that is how I sometimes am with God. My focus on my sin becomes a barrier between us, almost an idol, as I fixate more on my unworthiness than on God's love.

It's not about being a Good Girl, or a Bad Girl. It's about being God's girl, and spending time with Him, learning from Him and working with Him, being part of the family business as an heir, not a slave. It's about enjoying the abundance that comes from being part of the family as a blessing freely given, not a reward that must be earned. It's about enjoying God as my beloved Father, and rejoicing that I am His child, created and loved.

DIAMOND

I don't need to work to earn God's love. He loves me because I am His child.

Clarity
From the Word – A truth to stand on
For it is by grace you have been saved through faith, and this not from yourselves; it is the gift of God, not by works, so that no one can boast. Ephesians 2:8-9

Cut
Do you identify more with the older or the younger son in the parable? In what ways are you like them?
What happens when you focus more on your sin than God's love for you?

Colour
For your journal: Ask God to show you how your life would be different if you truly believed that you didn't need to *earn* His love or His forgiveness – that He wants you as His child, not for what you can do for Him.

Carat
Declaration: I am God's beloved child. I can't earn His love and I don't need to – He loves me because He made me.

Chapter 4

Growth

I sometimes feel so frustrated at the time it takes me to change. I have been walking with God for all my life, really, and yet I sometimes feel that I have barely begun to become who He wants me to be. I look at other people who seem to have achieved so much and I wonder what's wrong with me. When I was talking to God about this, about how frustrated He must be with me, He led me to think about parenting. He reminded me of the joy I had in my kids as they accomplished each new skill, even when they took time. It seemed He asked me if I would rather have had someone else bring up my kids for me and return them to me as adults, so that I avoided all the trouble. Of course, my answer was no! While parenting is so hard, I wouldn't give up a moment of it to get an 'instant' son or daughter.

As I reflected on God, I realised that He made a world where things start small and then grow. He could have created a finished universe where everything was complete, without capacity for change or growth. But He didn't. He seems to enjoy watching His creation develop. Perhaps that's one of the reasons He calls Himself our Father.

As I continued to pray, He reminded me of a collage painting that I had done with a group of children. We started by marbling paper – swirling colours together to make beautiful patterns. And we rejoiced over the beauty of the paper. Then we cut the paper into shapes and attached them to a canvas. Again, we rejoiced at the beauty we saw. Next, we decorated the picture with edges and highlights and embellishments. We were so excited at the new beauty revealed. Finally, we had the picture framed, and we rejoiced afresh, that we could make something so beautiful. God showed me how each stage was beautiful to me, even though it was not complete. I don't have to be afraid of boring God, or of making Him impatient. He loves me, and He has all the time in the world (or out of it) to form me as He desires. I'm the one in a hurry. I need to choose to trust Him with the process and enjoy the journey with Him.

In Ephesians 2:10, Paul says that we are God's workmanship. He has made us and He is growing us. Most good things take time to make and to develop, and usually rushing it only spoils it. When I feel like giving up or hiding because I am not satisfied with my progress I need to lean into Him and trust Him that He knows what He is doing. I don't know what God has planned for me to become. I am the pot, He is the Potter. A pot trying to form itself instead of submitting to the Potter's hands is not terribly useful. A pot deciding that it must be complete and jumping into the kiln limits what the Potter is able to do. I need to trust in God's plan for me.

I don't think God wants us to be passive in our growth, but He wants us to be responsive to Him, and to trust that He knows what He is doing. Of course, disobedience hinders growth, and needs to be confessed and repented of, but the need for growth is not just a result of sin. Even Jesus had to grow and mature. Luke tells us that, *"Jesus grew in wisdom and stature, and in favor with God and man."* (Luke 2:52).

Often I think our understanding of what God has planned for us is too small. In Ephesians 4:13 Paul talks about us maturing into the full stature of Christ. If that is His ultimate aim for us no wonder it takes so long. If I looked at the foundations of a massive high-rise being prepared and compared them to the foundations of a small cabin I would think that the high-rise was very slow. But only if I didn't know the intended final result. I love this quote from C. S. Lewis,

> "*Imagine yourself as a living house. God comes in to rebuild that house. At first, perhaps, you can understand what He is doing. He is getting the drains right and stopping the leaks in the roof and so on; you knew that those jobs needed doing and so you are not surprised. But presently He starts knocking the house about in a way that hurts abominably and does not seem to make any sense. What on earth is He up to? The explanation is that He is building quite a different house from the one you thought of - throwing out a new wing here, putting on an extra floor there, running up towers, making courtyards. You thought you were being made into a decent little cottage: but He is building a palace. He intends to come and live in it Himself.*"[1]

I have heard it said that God is easy to please but hard to satisfy. He is glad of each of our faltering steps towards maturity, but not satisfied until we reach the full stature of Christ. It is helpful if we can have the same attitude towards our own growth – if we can enjoy the process and trust Him to develop us as He wishes.

God deals with each of us as individuals – He is not running a school or a factory but a family. We can't compare our growth with others. For one thing, we never know the full story, the areas in which they are

---

[1] Lewis, C. S. 1976. *Mere Christianity*. Collins Fontana Books: Glasgow. Page 172.

struggling or the things that are easy for them. Also, when we compare, we either feel despondent or proud, neither of which help our growth!

So, let's enjoy the ride as we journey with God and allow Him to grow and change us. Let's trust in His wisdom and His goodness and His patience and look forward to what He will accomplish in us.

DIAMOND

God is not in a hurry. He loves me and He loves
to grow me into the full stature of Christ.

Clarity
From the Word – a truth to stand on
So Christ Himself gave the apostles, the prophets, the evangelists, the pastors and teachers, to equip His people for works of service, so that the body of Christ may be built up until we all reach unity in the faith and in the knowledge of the Son of God and become mature, attaining to the whole measure of the fullness of Christ. Ephesians 4:11-13

Cut
Are you impatient with yourself? What part of yourself would you most like God to 'fix'? Bring that to God and ask Him to show you how He sees it.

Colour
For your journal: Spend some time reflecting on your life. Ask God to show you how you have grown and changed in Him. Ask Him to remind you of things you thought would never change that are now just a memory. Thank Him for the journey.

Carat
Declaration: God will never give up on me. He loves me and He is not impatient with me. He is maturing me to the full measure of the stature of Christ!

SECTION 2

What am I?

Chapter 5

Matter Matters!

I enjoy my mind. Thinking gives me joy. Wrestling with an issue, debating it with my friends, reading different authors' opinions. I'm less happy with my body. I am tall – 176cm – and I grew tall very young. At ten I was a head taller than all my classmates, at twelve I was taller than most of my teachers. I was long and gangly, clumsy and uncoordinated. Clothes fit poorly, particularly as I was also very thin. To make matters worse, I was never any good at sports. Even though I was the tallest, I was always the last in every running race, and team ball games were torture – I would inevitably drop the ball and incur the wrath of my teammates. It turned out later that I had an eye issue with bi-focal vision, which meant I had very poor depth perception. Add to that early puberty, and I was never going to fit in well with my classmates. My body didn't seem to be my friend. It made me feel foolish and ashamed.

Perhaps because of the shame associated with my body, I had a very mind-centered theology. I considered myself a mind who happened to have a body, which I looked forward to losing in heaven. I didn't consider the physical as being very important, and if I'm honest, I probably thought that our physicality was part of our fallen condition, not an intentional, beautiful part of our creation.

In the last few years God has been using various means to show me that He made us physical beings because He wanted to. It wasn't a mistake. This amazing world we live in was not made just as a convenient place for our spirits to exist in until we left behind our bodies for good in eternity. God loves this physical universe that He created. He took great joy in crafting each element of it, and He plans to restore it all to what He intended it to be. This is referred to all through the Bible, but somehow, I never saw it. Revelation 21 speaks of a new heaven and a new earth, with no more suffering and no more death. Romans 8:19-23 talks of creation waiting with bated breath for its freedom from decay, for its restoration to its true purpose. Matter will be redeemed, not destroyed. Creation will come into its true relation with us when the curse that was put on it is lifted. It was cursed because of our sin, and our full restoration will also see it restored.

I find it so exciting to think of creation returning to how it was meant to be. Creation is so beautiful, and yet it is broken, just as our bodies, minds and spirits are broken. I wonder whether part of what we saw in Jesus' miracles was a foretaste of what it will be like when creation is restored. Even before His resurrection, Jesus was not limited by creation. If He needed more food, it was there. If He needed to get across a lake and He didn't have a boat, He simply walked, and the water became what He needed it to become. If He had water but wanted wine, then He had it. Inconvenient storms were calmed, and illness had no place with Him. He seemed to have a much more friendly relationship with creation than we have. After His resurrection it was even more evident. He was physically present but was unlimited by walls or distance. He seems to have been where He wanted to be, for as long as He wanted to be there. He was still able to be touched (John 20:27) and to touch (Luke 24:50), to breath (John 20:22) and to eat (Luke 24:42-43), but He doesn't seem to be constrained by those things. We are told that we will be transformed to be like Him, "*the Lord Jesus Christ, who, by the power that enables Him to subject all things to Himself, will transform our lowly bodies to be like His glorious body.*" (Phillipians 3:21). How wonderful it will be to be able to enjoy creation and our bodies as we were meant to, rather than in this limited, broken way we experience them now.

If we are to be bodies for eternity, then we should learn to worship God with our bodies, not just our minds and spirits. One way that God has been teaching me to do that is through dance. As a little girl I loved to dance. One of the best gifts I was ever given was a pink satin tutu my mother made for me when I was about seven. I loved that tutu so much. I felt beautiful in it, and one of the joys of my life is that it lasted long enough for my kids to dance in it as well.

But as I grew older and taller, my love of dancing became an embarrassment. I had always wanted to learn ballet, so when I was ten my mum enrolled me in a class. The trouble was that everyone else had been dancing since they were little, and I had no idea what I was doing. I felt useless and humiliated as I tried to keep up. I remember dancing joyfully at a school disco when I was eleven or twelve, and in my exuberance swinging my arms and hitting someone behind me. I felt like an elephant – there was much too much of me. I didn't have a good memory of steps, so doing aerobics (the latest craze when I was a teenager) in PE class at school made me feel so uncoordinated. Clearly, I wasn't meant to dance.

But slowly, gently, God has been restoring my love of movement. About ten years ago I bundled up all my courage and joined an adult ballet class. I felt useless at it, but I loved it; no one cared how well or poorly I moved, so I stuck at it, and slowly learned a little grace. I still have trouble remembering the steps, but I just stand at the back and copy someone, and it really doesn't matter.

Then God started challenging me to use my body to worship Him. First it was just raising my hands, then my arms in worship. Not very difficult, but at first, I felt so awkward. Then He asked me to kneel in church. At that time, that was a very odd thing in my church, and it took me a while to build up the courage to do it. Then one day our pastor was preaching on different expressions of worship and mentioned dancing. In the song after the sermon I felt compelled to go to the front and dance. It was so scary. I danced for one song, and then felt so incredibly embarrassed I couldn't turn around and go back to my seat, and so I just knelt at the front and hid my face (I can't remember how I eventually got back). Slowly, little step by little step, God has taught me to use my body to worship Him. He has shown me that I can dance prophetically, to change the atmosphere in the room. He has shown me that He can speak first to my body and use my body to speak to my mind and spirit. He has taught me to choose to worship with my body to lead my mind and spirit to a place of worship. It is such a blessing to me, and I have been told by many people that my dancing is a blessing to them as well. One comment a friend made was incredibly healing to me. She said that she never thought that a woman of my stature could move with such grace. What a sweet blessing, for a girl who saw herself as an elephant!

Another impact of my acceptance of matter as a good gift rather than a curse is that it changed my attitude towards the everyday. Suddenly routine activities like working and cooking and gardening and cleaning can become hallowed. Two things that we know about Adam and Eve in the Garden is that they walked and talked with God (Gen 3:8) and they gardened (Gen 2:15). Before I would have esteemed the former and seen the latter as spiritually insignificant. But God clearly values both. Work is regularly mentioned as a good in the Bible, and one of the blessings that we can anticipate in the new creation is that every person will be able to enjoy the fruits of their labour (Isaiah 65:21-23). The first mention we have in the Bible of someone being filled with the Holy Spirit is regarding work and creativity: *"And He has filled him with the Spirit of God, with skill, ability, and knowledge in all kinds of craftsmanship, to design artistic works in gold, silver, and bronze,"* (Exodus 35:31-32). We don't need to divide our lives into the sacred and the secular. Look how Jesus used the acts of washing and eating as gateways to Him, as He commanded us to be baptized and to remember Him in communion.

When we look at creation, we see how incredibly creative and artistic God is. Understanding that matter is good also freed me to be creative and to enjoy making things beautiful. Spending time painting a picture or sewing a dress is not a waste of time that could be spent in more 'holy' pursuits. If done with the right attitude, it is an aspect of my nature as one created in God's image.

Matter can be messy, but God made it for us. We are not just spirits who happen to inhabit bodies. Rather we are bodies, souls and spirits, and each part of us can worship God.

DIAMOND

God made matter and He likes it.

Clarity
From the Word – A truth to stand on
Love the Lord your God with all your heart and with all your soul and with all your mind and with all your strength. Mark 12:30

Cut
What do you think about your body? Do you see it as a good gift from God or do you resent or dislike it? It you can't honestly thank God for giving you your body, spend some time with God asking Him to show you how wonderful it is. Repent for your judgement of God, because He is the one who made your body.

Colour
For your journal: Do you use your body to worship God? Ask God to show you a way for you to worship with your body, not just your mind and spirit. It may be kneeling down, or raising your hands, or lying on your face before him, or even dancing. Try something new and ask God to speak to you through it.
Do you take time in your life to be creative? Ask God to remind you of something you loved to do when you were a kid, and try doing it again.

Carat
Declaration: My body is a good gift of God. Thank you, God, for making it.

Chapter 6

Glory

Have you ever noticed how often the Bible speaks about glory? It is such a common word in both the Old and New Testament, and yet it is one which we rarely speak about in church. I started to explore glory when I was overwhelmed by Hebrews 1:3, where it says that Jesus is the radiance of God's glory (I discuss this further in Chapter 21). I spent a long time trying to understand glory better. I read every reference to glory in the Bible and made my Bible Study group look at many of them as well. Finally, we came to the topic of glory in my theology class. I came to see that God's glory is His revelation of Himself, who He is and what He is like. He reveals His glory in everything He does. He does nothing that is not glorious. Through eternity He has been revealing His glory to Himself as the three-in-one God of the Trinity. Jesus prayed, *"Father, glorify me in your presence with the glory I had with you before the world began"* (John 17:5). He then chose to reveal His glory to the world through Jesus Christ. When we look at the life of Jesus, we see the glory of God made flesh. When we glorify God, we acknowledge the truth of who He is, how amazing and wonderful and awe-inspiring.

I still feel far from really being able to understand God's glory, but I was amazed at how many times **our** glory is referred to. There are so many references to us being glorified, or us having glory. It made me reflect more on what God has in mind for us as our eternal destiny. We were made for glory, and this life that we are living now is a pale reflection of what God intends for us.

Our tendency is to think that this is 'real life', and that when we die we go to the great retirement home in the sky, where nothing more is expected of us. But this is not real life. This is a war zone. It is like an alien landed in London in 1940 and thought that that was what life on earth was supposed to be like. That rationing and bombing and fear and death and families being separated was just the way that life was, and that winning the war was all that gave life meaning. We know that what happens during war is a fight to get back to real life. Wars are fought so that people can live in peace. We don't always recognise it, but we are fighting a war, we are living in a broken world. The way that we live is not 'normal'. It is not what we were designed for.

We think too little of ourselves. We were not made just to endure and survive. We were made to be glorified, to be sons of God (sons being heirs and participants in the family business, and carriers of the Father's authority, not just males), to be co-heirs with Christ, to attain the full stature of Christ. Glory is not just radiance. It is honour and authority. When death and decay are conquered, and the new heaven and new earth (Revelation 21:1-22:7) are revealed, our real life will begin. The rationing and pain and fear will be over. We will be able to invest our energy into what we were really made to do, instead of funnelling everything into the war effort. There will be work to do in the new earth.

But not the work of war. It will be creative and beautiful, full of glory and honour.

The more I meditate on the glory that is to come, for us and for creation, the more excited I get. This is not real life. This is not what we were made for. The good times are coming. We are heirs, we have great expectations. We need to stop living like paupers.

DIAMOND

We have an amazing destiny, living in glory with God.

Clarity
From the Word – A truth to stand on
I have given them the glory that You gave Me, that they may be one as We are one -I in them and You in Me—so that they may be brought to complete unity. Then the world will know that You sent Me and have loved them even as You have loved Me. John 17:22-23

Cut
How do you feel about being glorified? Does it seem presumptuous? Ask God if you're believing a lie about how He sees you.

Colour
For your journal: What do you think Jesus means when He says that He has given us glory? Ask Jesus to show you what sort of glory He gives us.

Carat
Declaration: God made us for glory. I don't have to make myself less to make Him more.

Chapter 7

Light

'You are the light of the world. A town built on a hill cannot be hidden. Neither do people light a lamp and put it under a bowl. Instead they put it on its stand, and it gives light to everyone in the house. In the same way, let your light shine before others, that they may see your good deeds and glorify your Father in heaven.
—Matthew 5:14-16

Jesus said to us, *'You are the light of the world'*. It is hard for us to appreciate what that really means, living as we do with as much light as we want at the click of a switch. But imagine what light meant in Jesus' time. If you've ever been camping, you probably have some idea.

When you are camping, there is an urgency as the day begins to fade. It is important to get things organised while you can still see well. I always want to get out everything for dinner, and make sure that the beds are ready to sleep in. But even camping, we have good torches, it is still easy to turn on light. Imagine what it was like to live with the only source of light being a little oil lamp. Darkness must have felt like an enemy. In the darkness, you were blind. Darkness meant danger. Darkness limited your ability to act. In the darkness, you were likely to stumble, to be lost. One time, Jesus remarked, *'Are there not twelve hours of daylight? Anyone who walks in the daytime will not stumble, for they see by this world's light. It is when a person walks at night that they stumble, for they have no light.'* (John 11:9-10).

John described Jesus' coming this way, *'In Him was life, and that life was the light of all mankind. The light shines in the darkness and the darkness has not overcome it.'* (John 1:4-5). Jesus came like light into a dark world. For those who accepted Him, He chased away the darkness. He gave the ability to see truly. He brought security and life.

It is easy for us to accept that Jesus was the light of the world. But what did He mean when He said that WE are the light of the world? I always pictured my light as small and flickering. A bit like a birthday candle – one little puff of wind could put it out. The lyrics of the old song, 'This little light of mine' didn't help. I remember singing it as a child holding up my finger to represent my light. How could a light like that make a difference?

One day as I was spending time with God I painted a picture. It started as a blaze of light, filling the whole sheet. In the very centre, where the light was brightest, I drew a small person. I asked God who the person was, expecting Him to say Jesus. But He didn't. He told me it was me. That my light is not a little flickering flame so small that it hardly changes the darkness, but that it is bright and powerful, because it comes from Him.

Because I didn't know the power of the light, I didn't use it. Because I believed that I was powerless, I was. This picture has made a big difference to me.

Of course, when Jesus said to His followers that they were the light of the world, He was speaking to all of them. I, individually, am not the light of the world, we are. But each of us carry God's light, and He commands us not to hide it.

I started to pray that God would make me light wherever I went. I particularly asked to be light in the state school where I was a chaplain. I was so encouraged when the deputy principle commented that I was the sunshine of the school, and when the registrar said that when I was there the whole atmosphere was different.

When you switch on the light, it doesn't have to struggle to make the darkness go away. Darkness disappears in the presence of light because darkness is an absence of light. I'm not saying that there is no such thing as spiritual warfare, but we need to know that we are on the winning team, and we don't need to be afraid.

Another aspect of being light comes from my meditation on Jesus being the radiance of God's glory (see Chapter 21 for a full discussion of this idea). Jesus is the light that shows us what the Father is like. But He also called us light. What if we are also meant to be radiance that shows people what the Father is like? Imperfectly of course. But haven't you heard it said that for many non-Christians, you are the only Bible they will read? If you are a Christian, God has made you light. Light to cast out darkness. And light to show those in the dark a glimpse of what a loving God looks like.

If you are a Christian, you can make a difference wherever you go. You (plural) are the light of the world. Ask God what that means in your life.

———————— DIAMOND ————————

We are the light of the world. God uses us to make a difference

Clarity
From the Word – A truth to stand on
'You are the light of the world. ... let your light shine before others, that they may see your good deeds and glorify your Father in heaven.' Matthew 5:14,16

Cut
Ask God to show you ways that you have limited His light in you.

Colour
For your journal: God, please show me how I am light to the world around me. Can you give me a picture of what my light looks like?

Carat
Declaration: I choose to believe Jesus when He says that I and all Christians are the light of the world. I will live trusting God to use me to bring His light into dark places.

Chapter 8

The Treasure and the Merchant

"The Kingdom of Heaven is like treasure hidden in a field. When a man found it, he hid it again, and then in his joy went and sold all he had and bought that field. "Again, the Kingdom of Heaven is like a merchant looking for fine pearls. When he found one of great value, he went away and sold everything he had and bought it.
—Matthew 13:44-46

Recently we had to sort through my mother-in-law's house, trying to decide what to do with a lifetime's possessions. Some decisions were easy – no one would want that broken cup kept for a rainy day – but others were difficult. We had no idea of the real value of things, what was valuable and what was just rubbish. We needed an expert to look at the treasures and help us to make decisions. But even then, when we came to selling things, the value was ultimately decided by what someone was prepared to pay.

The parables of the Treasure and the Merchant talk about the true value of things. About the value of the treasure, and the value of the pearl. Lots of people think that this is two parables saying the same thing, but as I meditated on them, I saw something different.

The first one says that the Kingdom of Heaven is like buried treasure. Imagine the scene. A man, probably a day labourer, is digging in a field. His spade hits something different from usual. As he tries to dig it out he realises that he has found something special. Treasure!! As he starts to uncover it he can't believe his luck. But then he realises that it is not his. If he takes it from the field he is a thief. But then he thinks, "What if I bought the field? If the field was mine the treasure would be mine. But how?" He quickly covers up the treasure and tries to act normal. When he goes home, he turns his life upside down. He sells everything he owns, his bed, his cooking equipment, his spare clothes; everything; and then he hurries to the owner of the field with every penny he can scrape together with an offer – he wants to buy the field. Clearly the owner has no idea that the treasure is there, so he sells it. Now the man can rush back to his field and dig up the treasure. He is richer than he ever imagined possible.

The man who found the treasure could never have bought it for himself. But he could (just) buy the field. Selling everything he had to buy the field was no great sacrifice. He sold his things in joy. When he sold his belongings to buy the field, he got rid of things of little worth to get something of great worth.

As I reflected on how this is like the Kingdom of Heaven. I thought that the man represents us, and the treasure represents our relationship with God. The man didn't earn the treasure – it came to him free of charge. His was not the work that accumulated it. It wasn't his by inheritance. He could never provide it for himself. But, he had to take action to get it. He had to give up everything, not to buy the treasure, but to get access to it. We can't earn the right to enter the Kingdom of God.

It doesn't matter how hard we try, we can never become good enough to save ourselves. We can't inherit our place in the kingdom of heaven from our parents or achieve it by going to church. We can only receive this most valuable of privileges as a free gift of God. And yet, it is not without cost to us. We can't follow Jesus and continue to live our old life. Being a follower of Jesus changes everything, costs us everything. It changes how we spend our money and our time. It changes our dreams and our goals. Jesus said in Luke 9:24-25 *"For whoever wants to save their life will lose it, but whoever loses their life for me will save it. What good is it for someone to gain the whole world, and yet lose or forfeit their very self?"*

I find this parable so helpful. It helps me to understand how something can be free and yet costly at the same time.

What about the pearl? On the surface it seems the same. Someone finds something valuable and gives all that they have to get it. But the wording of this one is different. In the first one the Kingdom is like a treasure. In the second one the Kingdom is like a merchant. The merchant is an expert, who spends his life looking for the most beautiful pearls. Pearls in the ancient world were the most valuable of gems, which is why Cleopatra famously dissolved one in her wine to make the most expensive dinner party ever. A rare pearl could be almost priceless, worth millions if not billions of dollars.

So, this merchant is actively searching for pearls. He doesn't just happen to find a beautiful pearl as he is going about his business. His search is intentional and costly. He knows pearls, and he knows what they are worth. He is prepared to go to great lengths to find them. Imagine his excitement when he finds this very special pearl. The one for which he had been searching for so long. He had seen many pearls, he was an expert in pearls, but he had never seen one like this. He knew what it was worth, and he was prepared to pay it, even though it cost him everything he had. And so he sold all his beautiful possessions, just to buy this one pearl.

Can you imagine how he would have felt when he owned the pearl? How he would have gloated over it and enjoyed it? How he would have shown it to his friends and pointed out its special features? How he would have rejoiced to finally own the pearl of his dreams? Somehow, this one pearl was worth the price it cost, even though it cost him everything.

As I reflected, I came to the conclusion that it is not the same parable told twice. Being of scientific mind, I made a table to compare them:

Treasure	Merchant
Found by accident	He is searching for the pearl
Man is poor	He is rich
He pays a fraction of the cost of the treasure	He pays the full cost of the pearl
There is no real sacrifice	There is great sacrifice

As you can see, the two are quite different. So how is the merchant like the kingdom of heaven? I think that the merchant represents God, and we are the pearl for which He is prepared to sell everything. God gave up that which was most precious to Him – His only Son – to win us back to Himself. He did it intentionally and at great cost.

God says we are valuable. We know that by the price that He was prepared to pay for us. God is the ultimate expert as to the value of things. If He says that we are worth the life of His only Son, then He must be right, even though it is so hard to us to believe.

When we know the value of something it changes the way that we treat it. If we think something has no value then we don't treasure it or look after it carefully. Imagine if you had an old bowl that you used for scraps, and then a visitor came over and told you that it was a rare antique that was worth thousands. I bet you wouldn't use it for scraps any more!

I need to be reminded of my value often. As I have already shared, it is so easy for me to believe the lie that I am rubbish. It is as if I think that the merchant gave everything he had and in exchange got a plastic bead worth nothing, and then made everyone pretend that it was a beautiful pearl.

Knowing that I am valuable to God, that He sees me as beautiful and worth saving is such a blessing. Knowing that He sees everyone else the same way can be challenging. Every person I meet is a pearl of great price, for whom God was prepared to pay the life of His Son. There are no worthless people. The people I find most difficult or annoying are still people that God sees as pearls, and He is the expert. This, too, is a truth I need to be reminded of often. And it should spur me to evangelism. Jesus has paid His life to win each person – how tragic that He doesn't get all that He paid for.

DIAMOND

God sees us as pearls of great price, for whom He was prepared to pay the life of His Son.

Salvation is like a buried treasure. We can never pay for it, but we do have to choose to take it, and doing so means letting go of things that we formerly valued.

Clarity
From the Word – A truth to stand on
Indeed, the very hairs of your head are all numbered. Don't be afraid; you are worth more than many sparrows. Luke 12:7

Those of you who do not give up everything you have cannot be my disciples. Luke 14:33

Cut
Are you trying to have both the treasure and your old life? Ask God if there are things that He wants you to give up. Ask Him to show you ways that you are not living according to your true value. What would He like you to change?

Colour
For your journal: Which of these two parables are you more drawn to? Why? Ask God to show you ways in which He sees you as a pearl of great price.

Carat
Declaration: Lord, thank you that I am a pearl of great price to You. Help me to hold on to your treasure, and not the treasure of the world.

Chapter 9

The Image of the Lord

But we all, with unveiled face, beholding as in a mirror the glory of the Lord, are being transformed into the same image from glory to glory, just as from the Lord, the Spirit.
—*2 Corinthians 3:18 ASV*

Do you ever find that you are reading the Bible and suddenly a verse leaps out at you, perhaps one that you have read many times before, and it is like it is written for you alone? God did that for me with this verse a few years ago. When I read '*beholding as in a mirror the glory of the Lord*' I was overwhelmed. How could I see the glory of God in a mirror? When I look in a mirror I see flaws – wrinkles and spots and imperfections. What on earth was Paul talking about? My reflections on this verse seem like a good summary of this first section of the book.

First, as Christians we come to God with unveiled faces. We don't need to have a veil or barrier between us and God. The veil that Paul mentions here is a reference back to the veil that was in the temple between the people and the Holy of Holies. When Jesus died, the veil was torn from top to bottom (Matt 27: 50-51), symbolizing that because of Jesus' sacrifice, we can freely come into God's presence.

Under the Law there was a separation between the people and God. That barrier is still there is you are not a Christian. If we have not accepted Christ's gift of forgiveness, then there is a barrier between us and God. It is hard for us to see God. He is hidden from us, and we tend to try to hide ourselves from Him. But when we become Christians, that veil is taken away. We can come to God face to face. We don't have to come to God with a mask on, pretending to be someone we're not. We don't have to be afraid of rejection or separate ourselves from God.

I realised, though, that I tended to put the veil back. Not the heavy veil that was there before I came to faith, but a veil of pretense and shame. As I discussed earlier, I was pretty sure that God didn't like the real me, and I had to pretend to be someone that I wasn't, so He could love me. Being totally real with God seemed too risky. I felt ashamed of who I really was, and so I metaphorically put on my 'Sunday best' when I entered His presence. I was like a petitioner entering into the court of a king rather than a child coming to her Daddy.

But I didn't need that veil. God loves me just as I am. He doesn't want me to pretend with Him, just as parents don't want their kids to feel that they have to dress up to come into their presence.

The next section of the verse says, *'Beholding as in a mirror the glory of the Lord'*. The Greek word that Paul used for beholding (katoptrízomai) is an uncommon one, and this is its only occurrence in the Bible. Where it is used in other Greek texts, it always carries a meaning of reflecting or observing in a mirror.

I asked God to show me how I could possibly behold His glory as in a mirror. He showed me a couple of things. First, my physical body. Why is it that for many of us, our biggest emotion regarding our body is shame? We look at ourselves and think that we are too fat or have too many wrinkles or too many pimples or are too short or tall or whatever.

And yet we didn't make our bodies. They are a gift of God. The Bible says that we are fearfully and wonderfully made. When I reflect on my body, it is amazing. I understand so little of it, and yet it performs its many and varied functions, without any conscious input from me.

Our bodies truly are a gift of God. I should look at my body and see the glory of God, the wonder of His creative and His sustaining power and His incredible generosity in giving me such an amazing gift. I should stand in awe of my body's ability to experience pleasure and to serve and to love and to reproduce; its ability to heal itself, to take random food and turn it into energy, to balance on two feet and even dance and sing. I should rejoice in the complex network of nerves that transfer information throughout the body at lightning speed, and all the amazing organs that work together to balance all my needs.

And if we are Christians our bodies are a temple of the Holy Spirit. God himself lives in them. Temples are not a hovel thrown together. They are beautiful, crafted, valuable places, used to show the glory of the God they honour. If our bodies are God's temple, then they have incredible value and worth.

So, God showed me the lie that I was believing when I saw my body as a thing of shame, that I could resent or want to hide away. But then He showed me that this went much deeper than just my body.

When I engage in self-reflection, I certainly don't tend to see the glory of God. I see failure and weakness and inadequacy. I see all the things that I don't like about myself. But we're told in Genesis 1:27 that God created us in His image. God made each of us unique with our own personalities and gifts and abilities. But in some way that we don't fully understand we each are in His image. Just like we didn't make our bodies we didn't make our souls or our spirits. They are gifts and creations of the most high God, and when we look at them we should see not just our failures but His glory.

Of course, mirrors in the ancient world were not like our mirrors today. They were polished metal and would have given a somewhat distorted reflection. And this is true of us. We don't fully and accurately reflect God's glory. In Romans 3:23 Paul says that all of us have sinned and fallen short of the glory of God. None of us are righteous in ourselves, all of us were sinners from birth. But when we became Christians, that changed. Paul goes on to say that we all are justified freely by His grace through the redemption that came by Christ Jesus. The Bible says many things about our state after our salvation that I often find very difficult to believe. It says that we are new creations, sons and daughters of God able to call Him Daddy, co-heirs with Christ, being transformed into His likeness, justified and made righteous in His sight. The list could go on and on.

In Romans 8:1 Paul makes an amazing statement which we have discussed before. He says there is no condemnation for those who are in Christ Jesus. If there is now no condemnation for us who are in Christ Jesus, why do we look at ourselves with condemnation? In Revelation 12:10 it says that Satan is the accuser of the brethren. If we look at ourselves with self-accusation, whose voice are we listening to? We know that it is not God's, as He says that there is no condemnation. Satan is the accuser and the deceiver. He is the one who wants to condemn us. We have a choice of who to believe. I can ask God to show me His glory that is reflected in me, or I can listen to Satan's voice telling me how useless I am. If I feel under condemnation, I know that I am not listening to God.

This doesn't mean that I think that I don't sin, and that I don't have to confess my sin. Of course, I do. But it is about my core beliefs about myself and God. Do I see myself as a sinner, a piece of rubbish who occasionally does something good, or do I see myself as God says that I am, a new creation, justified and righteous, who sometimes sins? A young friend of mine who loved God and was active in His service shared with me about his struggles with pornography, and the sense that he had was that the real him was the man hunched over the screen, not the Christian sharing the gospel and leading the youth. He felt that God confronted him and told him that the real him was the one serving God, the sinner was the old man passing away. He wasn't being a hypocrite serving God while there was still sin in his life. That change of belief actually helped him to get free of pornography, as he saw that it didn't reflect who he truly was.

The verse goes on to say that as we behold the glory of God as in a mirror, we are being transformed into that same image from one degree of glory to another. There are several powerful concepts in those few words.

The first concept I see in this is tension between what is and what will be. We are made in the image of God, and we look in the mirror and see His glory, but we are not completed. We are on a journey. All the things that I said earlier are true, but they are not finished. The Greek word used here for transform (metamorphoomai) is the word we get metamorphosis from. It is a sense of a complete change, inside and out. While we are on this earth we are being transformed, but the transformation has not fully occurred.

We see this tension between the 'now' and the 'not yet' through the Bible. For example, in Romans 8:15 Paul talks about our adoption as God's children as something that has already occurred, and in Romans 8:23 he says it is something we are waiting for. As I wrestled with this tension, God reminded me of pregnancy. A newly pregnant woman is, in one sense, a mother. She has conceived a child. And yet we are not mistaken in calling her an 'expectant' mother. Her maternity is both a current fact and a future hope, but a hope in which she can be confident, because she experiences that firstfruits of her maternity in her body. In the same way we are truly already children of God. We can be confident in our status because the Holy Spirit dwells within us. But we have not fully received our adoption. It is both a current fact and a future hope.

And so this verse speaks of us *being* transformed. It is a process. We are not yet what we will be. We already have some glory, but there will be more and more glory for us, as God continues to transform us. For we are not transforming ourselves, but God is transforming us. We are His workmanship, and He is growing in us the fruit of the Spirit. Jesus told His disciples in John 15 that He was the vine and they were the branches, and that if they stayed connected to Him they would bear much fruit, but by themselves they could do nothing. A grape branch bears grapes because it is its nature to bear grapes and because it receives all it needs from the vine. We don't need to stress and strain to bear fruit, we just need to stay connected to Jesus. He will transform us.

I find this a bit counter intuitive. I feel as though it is my job to work hard to turn myself into the person I am supposed to be. And it is true that I can get in the way of my transformation. But ultimately, this is not our job. The main agent of our transformation is God. We can do nothing without Him. But we can cooperate or not. We can contemplate or not. We can open ourselves to Him or not. Just as we have no capacity to make a seed grow, but we can make the environment good or bad for its growth, we can't make ourselves grow, but we can set up an environment in ourselves that hinders or helps it. We can be good soil or poor soil.

This verse also talks about us going from glory to glory. As I discussed in the previous chapters, glory is not a topic we talk about much, even though it is all through the Bible. When we do think about glory it tends to be in relation to God. But here glory is for us.

Part of me recoils from this. Aren't we supposed to become less? But then I think of myself as a parent. I want my children to become more and more themselves. When they are honoured, I am honoured. Their glory doesn't diminish mine, it enhances it. God made us, after all. If He glorifies us, then we are more able to glorify Him.

What do we do with this? In Romans 12 Paul tells us to be transformed by the renewing of our minds. What we think matters. If we believe we are useless rubbish, we will tend to remain that way. We need to continually remind ourselves of what God says about us. There are so many verses that say things about us that seem audacious. When you read the Bible, write them down with your name in them. For example, read aloud Ephesians 1:3-14 saying your name where is says you, and ask God to reveal the truth of it to you.

DIAMOND

Because of what Jesus has done for us, God reveals His glory in us. We need to believe what God says about us and trust in Him to transform us.

Clarity
From the Word – A truth to stand on
For He chose us in Him before the creation of the world to be holy and blameless in His sight. In love He predestined us for adoption to sonship through Jesus Christ, in accordance with his pleasure and will. Ephesians 1:4-5

Cut
Do you feel condemned? Do you believe what God says about you if you are a Christian, or are you listening to the accuser? Ask God to show you if you are believing a lie about yourself or God.

Colour
For your journal: Write out some of the amazing verses saying how God sees us. Speak these truths over yourself, and choose to trust that God knows what He is talking about when He describes you.

Carat
Declaration: I choose to listen to what the Bible says about me. I will not listen to the lies that Satan tells me. I am righteous and beloved because of Christ's work for me.

Diamonds From Experience

Lessons learned from life

SECTION 3

Where's God When Life Hurts?

Chapter 10

Overlooked

Every day it was the same. Walking around the school quadrangle, eating my lunch and pretending to look for my friends. Sitting alone was too weird, and I had no one to sit with, so I went through this sad pretense until the library opened and I could go there.

School for me was a difficult experience. I loved learning, so the schoolwork was not a problem. But socially, I was lost. I didn't seem to know the magic words that everyone else knew. I didn't know how to respond when someone teased me. I wasn't interested in the same things as everyone else, and physically I was a total clutz with no dress sense. I was the one picked last for every team, the one who dropped the ball or tripped over at the crucial time. I was that classic nerd girl in all the movies, lost and alone.

My transformation did come in time. Not the big dramatic one where someone took off my glasses and did my hair and the star of the football team fell in love with me. But as I entered my senior years at high school, I started to find likeminded people, who liked to discuss 'deep and meaningfully' or D & M as we called it, who were interested in history or science or philosophy, and who didn't care if I couldn't catch a ball. I started to develop friendships, and so I learned how to be a friend.

As an adult, friendship is no longer an issue. I have many wonderful friends. But the long years of being left out and overlooked left their mark. I am very sensitive to the feeling of being the odd one out. When I experience that I need to intentionally manage my feelings, so as to not allow offence to enter my heart. It has also made me very sensitive to disappointment. One thing that used to happen periodically at school was that I would be allowed into a friendship group. For a few days, I would have people to sit with - I would be included. But then the friendship would be withdrawn. Perhaps I would transgress the rules in some way. Or it suited the Queen Bee girl to push me out again. This blowing hot and cold was so painful. Feeling hopeful that this time it would be different, that this time I had a place, only to have it snatched away again. Even worse, I had to pretend that I didn't care, because displaying weakness only gave them another way to attack me.

The temptation of repeated disappointment is to close your heart to hope. Why hope when it will only lead to pain? But, as I discuss in the next chapter, hope is highly commended in the Bible. Paul says, *'These three things remain, Faith, Hope and Love.'* (1 Corinthians 13:13). To give up on hope is to close yourself off, shutting the doors of your heart and refusing to allow anyone in. Even God is kept out, because, ultimately, who has more capacity to disappoint than God? He promises so much and yet at times He seems to fail to deliver.

I think the experience of being bullied and excluded in school has also contributed to my fear of being overlooked by God. I struggle not to feel left out when I am not chosen for a role or a task. It is so tempting to look at other peoples' journeys and feel envious. But each person's journey is unique, and each have their own challenges which are often hidden. I need to keep coming back to God, repenting for judging Him and for not trusting Him to be working for my good. I need to choose hope over despair. I need to take risks, knowing that I might be disappointed, but taking them anyway, trusting God to have it in hand.

But God has also brought blessing from that time. It taught me to be self-reliant, because I had no one else to lean on. I had lots of adventures that I wouldn't have had if I had always needed a group to do things with. He taught me to see the overlooked people, and to have compassion. Somehow it taught me to be comfortable in my own skin, because I learnt not to rely on other peoples' affirmation all the time. If I thought something was right I would do it. And I read a lot of good books!

All of us have hurts from our childhood, whether from friends or parents or life. None of us grow up without wounds. Being aware of those wounds is helpful, because our response to wounding tends to send us in characteristic directions. Part of the journey to maturity is knowing our instinctive responses to pain and learning how to manage them. God can and does heal us as we forgive those who hurt us and repent of our sinful responses to hurt, but for many of us those tendencies remain. When I seem to be over-reacting to something, I ask God what the lie is that I am believing, and whom I need to forgive. Knowing the way that I tend to respond gives me power over it. I can choose not to agree with the lie that I learnt as a child, and I can choose to rely on the truth that God has shown me.

—— DIAMOND ——

Understanding our past can help us to live more richly in the present.

Clarity
From the Word – A truth to stand on
No, in all these things we are more than conquerors through Him who loved us. Romans 8:37

Cut
Ask God to bring to mind any deep hurts from your past that are still affecting you now. What are the characteristic lies that you tend to believe? (Sometimes it can be helpful to talk this sort of thing through with a trained counsellor).

Colour
For your journal: Ask God to reveal to you the truths that you can stand on when those lies come to mind.

Carat
Declaration: I am not my past. I do not have to continue to repeat the patterns I learned as a child. When I find myself doing so, I choose to turn to God, and ask Him to remind me of His truth and to empower me to live in it.

Chapter 11

Mum

Mostly life just goes on, day by day. But there are those other days; days when everything changes. These are days that become marking stones in our lives. As I look back on my life, there are the days that stand out. The day I asked Rob (my husband) to go out with me. The day I left home. The days I found out I was pregnant. One of those days for me was 27th September 1985. That was the day I found out that Mum had cancer; the day I stopped believing that nothing really bad could happen to us. It was the day I started to learn that when the things you fear really do happen, that God will give you the strength you need to get through each day.

For a long time, if you asked me to tell you one fact about myself, I would tell you that my mother died. It was impossible for you to know me if you didn't know that fact. Life was in three parts – before Mum got sick, while she was sick, and after she died.

From when Mum was about 40 until she was 44, she kept going to different doctors telling them that there was something wrong. She was given different vague diagnoses – irritable bowel, varicose veins on the stomach, prolapsed uterus, even a referral to a psychologist as it was thought that she was trying to get attention as her identity as a mum to little kids had changed– but no real answers. Diagnostic techniques were less developed in the 80s, and nothing showed in the scans. Her father was a specialist physician, well-known for finding answers when no-one else could, but he was as lost as anyone. Finally, the gynecologist agreed to do a laparoscopic investigation, more to shut Mum up than anything.

By this time, Mum was convinced that there was nothing serious, so she decided to have the procedure done while Dad was in Europe for work so as not to inconvenience him. She drove herself to the hospital, and I drove the car home since I worked only a few hundred metres away from the hospital. At this time, I had just turned 22, and my three younger brothers were 19, 16 and 14.

The next morning will be forever engraved in my memory. Before I went to work, I took a phone call from my grandfather. He told me that there was something seriously wrong with Mum, but not to tell her or my younger brothers. I can't remember his words, but for some reason I was convinced she had a strange, tropical disease. Cancer never crossed my mind, and I certainly never considered that she might die. But it was still upsetting – I could never remember my mum being sick, and so I started to cry. One of my brothers wanted to know what was wrong, but I wasn't allowed to tell him, so I tried to convince him that there was something in my eye! Before work, I popped in to see Mum. It was awful. No one had spoken to her, so she was saying that it must be nothing serious or the doctor would have spoken to her by now. I had to smile and pretend to agree.

At work that morning my Granny (Mum's mum) rang me. She said something about Mum's cancer, and I was horrified. When I told her I didn't know that Mum had cancer, she tried to tell me a bit more, but at that stage no one really knew much. Just that there were abnormal cells her abdomen, and that they would have to do major surgery to try to get rid of it.

Poor Dad was in Sweden, and had a horrible, forty-eight-hour journey to get home, as he couldn't get good connections. Because of this, it was up to me to tell my brothers and to call Mum's friends. It was hard, but as I repeated the information over and over, and absorbed people's shocked reactions the truth of it started to sink in.

Mum had a few days home, and then went back for her surgery. They thought it was ovarian cancer, so they planned a full hysterectomy as well as debulking her abdomen. However, when they went in they were very surprised that it was cancer of the appendix. This is an extremely rare cancer, so they had no real prognosis for how long she was likely to live and no standard treatment.

Sitting by Mum's bedside, holding her hand as we waited for her to come around from the anesthetic, Dad and I prayed for Mum. It was a peaceful time, though we feared the future.

I went into helper mode. I tried to do everything Mum would usually do, as well as working full time and visiting her three times a day. Not only were there my three brothers to look after (I even made their lunches as Mum always had), but there were also so many pets. Dog, cats, chickens, a variety of birds, even rapidly growing and very hungry silkworms. Hundreds of silkworms. Mum was very tender hearted with animals, and didn't like to destroy any eggs, so every year we had more and more silkworms. Part of my daily routine was bringing home a branch of mulberry leaves. It was all very exhausting.

Where was God in this? I had been a Christian since I was a little girl, but my faith had never really been tried by anything before. I was relieved to find that it could stand the test. God drew closer, and the verse Romans 8:28 became my lifeline, *'And we know that in all things God works for the good of those who love Him, who have been called according to His purpose.'* I clung to that, and trusted that God would work good in this. As Mum recovered and struggled to come to terms with what was happening to her, she often turned to me for answers. I spent many hours reading and wrestling with questions about heaven and God's ways. The books of C. S. Lewis were my biggest help at this time, but God sent many other helps. Mum and I were both encouraged by a dear friend, Julie, whom we both deeply admired, whose mum had died about ten years earlier when Julie was around my age. We could see that this experience had not destroyed her, though she still grieved. We took hope from that. There were so many good friends who gathered around and prayed and talked and gave practical assistance. People who would listen to us, weep with us, share our pain, our hopes and our fears. People who cooked meals, cleaned the house, drove Mum to appointments. There were other peoples' stories of sickness and loss, of healing and of grace. I looked everywhere for answers. Answers never really came, but God did, and He was present in the midst of it all.

For the first 6 months or so we had hope. Maybe the cancer was all gone. Maybe Mum would get better or would live a long life managing the condition. But then it became obvious that it was getting worse. She started getting more tumors in her abdomen, and her ability to absorb food became increasingly compromised. She became thinner and weaker and sicker.

Around this time, I came home from work one day and Mum was full of news. She had met with some friends who had kids who were working in Canberra, and she thought I should move there too. I was confused. How could I move to Canberra from Brisbane when Mum was so sick? It was so far away. I had imagined that I would live at home until Mum died, as she and the family needed me. But she could see more clearly. As the only girl in a family of boys, and the eldest, I was too likely to take on responsibilities that weren't mine. She didn't want me to spend the rest of her life, however long that was, with my life on hold. So, she gave me the most generous gift I have ever been given – she set me free.

I didn't really want to go, but as an obedient daughter I did as I was told and applied for jobs in Canberra. Soon enough I got one, and I was on my way. The farewells were horrible, and as a not-terribly-confident homebody the idea of starting a new life on my own was scary, but it seemed to be the right thing to do. As soon as I settled into a share house Mum came down to visit. She delighted in buying things for my house and planting some pansies and other flowers in my garden. She went on to live another ten months or so, but she was never well enough to come again. That was her one chance to help one of her birds fly the nest, and it is a blessing to remember.

I spent all my spare money and spare time travelling up to Brisbane – in those days it took two flights and several hours. It was always so hard to leave again. I hated that I wasn't the one nursing Mum as she got weaker, and I lived with constant fear of a phone call saying come home quickly. But both Mum and I knew that I was in the right place. Those last few months were full of ups and downs, though mostly downs, and it was hard going. We constantly prayed for a miracle.

Even though Mum's two and a half years of dying were terribly hard for all of us, especially her, they were so full of blessing. Mum had always struggled with low self-esteem and had not felt very loved by her parents (though they loved her dearly). Now she was lavished with love, and everyone made sure that they told her what she meant to them. She was amazed at the impact her life had had on people and treasured the feeling of being loved by her parents. Mum had always struggled to show physical affection. Now she reached out with loving touches at every opportunity. God came very close to her and to us during that time, and she lost her fear of death, though she loved life and didn't want to leave it.

For me, too, the fear of death was taken away. Most people in their early twenties never think of death, but for me it was a daily companion.

Seeing God's reality in that was amazing. I used to be so afraid of talking to people who were suffering, not knowing what to say. Mum's illness removed that entirely. I used to think that if something really bad happened that I wouldn't be able to cope, and so I was afraid. Experiencing one of my worst fears and finding that God was enough was incredibly liberating. Somehow, making that journey of illness, death and grief with God strengthened my faith immensely. It was as if there was a strong foundation that I knew nothing could shake. My faith had been through the fire and had come out the other side stronger and deeper. In Mum's last months I often thought that I didn't regret her cancer diagnosis as it gave so many gifts, but I longed for her to be healed, so she didn't have to die.

It wasn't to be. On 27 February 1988 mum slipped peacefully away, just two weeks after her 47th birthday. The funeral was beautiful, and I remember exalting in the statement that Mum had left the church militant and joined the church triumphant. But as the days turned into weeks and the weeks turned into months it became harder. I had had enough of grief. Couldn't we go back to normal? Of course, there is no going back. Over the years, my grief for Mum has become less, but more than 30 years on I still miss her. Every life event is made a little less because she is not there to share it. She would still only have been 80 – not very old by today's standards. My grief has two components. One is missing her, her presence in my life, and the joy that sharing my life with her would have brought. The other is grieving for what she is missing out on and would have so enjoyed, like becoming a grandmother and a great grandmother.

Losing my Mum so early has forever changed me. It has brought deep sorrow, not just for me but for my kids who missed out on having a wonderful Granny in their lives. However, it has also brought great blessing, for which I am thankful. It has taken away my fear of death, and of the dying. I have been privileged to walk the journey of dying with a number of people and have been able to do that without fear because of Mum. I have lived all my adult life with a deep knowing of my own mortality. That is a mixed blessing, but the truth is that we are all going to die, and none of us know how long we will be on this earth. I count myself blessed that I have not lived in the illusion that nothing will ever happen to me. I think I have relished life more and embraced it more fully than I would have done if I had not lost Mum. This knowing forced me to deeply contemplate eternity, and to explore teachings on what happens after we die. There is also a strength that comes with enduring your greatest fear and coming out the other side - a knowing that God will be with you, whatever comes.

Another favorite verse from Romans 8 (my favorite chapter of the Bible!) is 8:18 *'I consider that our present sufferings are not worth comparing with the glory that will be revealed in us.'* No matter what we suffer in this life, if we are Christians we know that it is nothing in comparison with what is to come for us, the glory that God has prepared for us. Suffering is part of life in this broken world of ours. We can't escape it. But we can be blessed in it and through it. Of course, God can and does heal us. But we don't have to be afraid of suffering. Romans 8:35-39 is incredibly comforting.

> *Who shall separate us from the love of Christ? Shall trouble or hardship or persecution or famine or nakedness or danger or sword? As it is written:*
> *'For your sake we face death all day long;*
> *we are considered as sheep to be slaughtered.'*
> *No, in all these things we are more than conquerors through Him who loved us. For I am convinced that neither death nor life, neither angels nor demons, neither the present nor the future, nor any powers, neither height nor depth, nor anything else in all creation, will be able*

to separate us from the love of God that is in Christ Jesus our Lord.

This life is fleeting and at times difficult. Taking the time to really get to know what you believe and in whom you are believing is such a help when the hard times come. For me, the foundation that I built as I struggled with Mum's illness and death has been a wonderful source of strength as I have faced other trials and losses. I encourage you to take the time to build that foundation now, whether or not you are currently in a time of suffering.

———————— DIAMOND ————————

God is enough. Though sometimes we suffer, He will never leave nor forsake us. Nothing that happens to us will be wasted.

Clarity
From the Word – A truth to stand on
And we know that in all things God works for the good of those who love Him, who have been called according to His purpose.
Romans 8:28

Cut
What is your greatest fear? Do you believe that God is strong enough even for that?

Colour
For your journal: Ask God to remind you of ways that He has been faithful to you in the past, and unexpected ways that He has worked for your good in and through difficult times. Record these things in your journal and look back at them when you feel discouraged.

Carat
Declaration: God, I choose to believe that whatever happens You will be there. I release my fears to You, trusting that You will be enough. Thank you for Your faithfulness.

Chapter 12

Grief

I remember standing on our front veranda, crying, as I struggled with Mum's illness and probable death. I felt so overwhelmed by it all. I suddenly remembered the verse from Isaiah where it prophesied that Jesus would be "*a man of sorrows, and acquainted with grief*" (Isaiah 53:3, KJV). I felt strangely comforted to know that now I too was acquainted with grief. Sadly, grief is an acquaintance that you never lose.

There has been much written about the stages of grief. My experience was much more circular than stages. It seemed that each stage was visited multiple times in various orders. Grief began with Mum's diagnosis and was intensified by her death. It was full of so many different feelings. One of the challenges of grief is that people grieve differently, and so the ones you are grieving with, who you would think would be your companions on the road, are often in a very different place from you. This led to some conflict and hurt in the family as one person might be in a denial stage and another in acceptance while a third might be angry and shut down, and each thought that the others didn't understand.

There are moments that stand out. Mum took a long time to die, as she was young and healthy in every way apart from the cancer. Living in a different city there was months of anxiety waiting for a bad news phone call. In the days before mobile phones, it was so much harder. I tried to make sure that I was always contactable, leaving messages about where I would be. Then finally, the call came at 2am one Saturday night. There was such a confusion of feelings: sorrow, relief, busyness. I needed to get on the first plane I could, so frantic phone calls were made. I don't remember the trip, but I remember being at the hospital with my family, seeing Mum's body for the last time. I hadn't realised how quickly death changes the appearance of the body – in some ways it was comforting that it was so clear that Mum was no longer present. I also made the discovery that grief doesn't shut out all other emotions, or not for very long. One of the comforts that God sends us in our grief is the mundane activities of life. Even in grief, food needs to be eaten, decisions need to be made, and flashes of joy or laughter can come. When I imagined grieving, I imaged that grieving would be all that I could do, and there were times that that was true. But mostly grieving is mixed in with other things.

In some ways the first weeks of grieving are easier than what comes after. No one expects you to go to work, and you are surrounded by loving people. There are many tears, but there are people to comfort you. We were surrounded by flowers (so many flowers!) and given meals and care. Going back to Canberra and work a week later was hard. I hoped that life would go back to normal, but of course it doesn't. I was frequently hit by unexpected tears. There was one awful day a few weeks in when I went to work and started crying, and just couldn't stop. I ended up having to go home.

There were unexpected helps. I remember a friend coming over and just crying with me. I think she felt bad that she lost control, but I was comforted. I read books about other people's grief experiences and found that helpful. I had a dear friend Sue who never met my Mum, but who was willing to listen as I spoke at length and repeatedly about some of the traumatic experiences of her death. I am a verbal processor, so having a friend who would listen not just once but repeatedly was an incredible blessing.

I had expected that the grief would be more or less done, in a year, but that was very unrealistic. A week before the first anniversary of Mum's death Rob and I got married. It was beautiful, but hard to be a bride without my Mum there. Rob lived in Melbourne, so I moved there to be with him, and shortly after returning from our honeymoon we bought our first home. That first year of marriage was challenging. I was continually sick. My body was completely overloaded with stress. Not only had I lost my Mum, I had also moved town twice, changed job twice, been in my first serious relationship (with a bloke who lived eight hours' drive away), gotten engaged, organised a wedding in a different city – Brisbane – in five months without the internet or a Mum to help me, and then bought a house. It was crazy. I was weepy and fragile – my reserves were all used up. It took quite a long time to recover (and then I got pregnant… but that's another story!). Grief is work, and a wise person tries to not to make any major life decisions in that first year or so. I had a major fail on that one!

In some ways the grief was a harder challenge to my faith than Mum's illness. When she was alive there was something to focus on, something to do. After she died there was a blank. But like all suffering, grief presents us with a choice. Do we lean into God or away from Him? There were times when I raged at God, yelling my despair and heart break, swearing and weeping, but He was always there. I felt safe and heard in my fury, and as it subsided He comforted me.

I became a mother three years after Mum's death. It brought a whole new layer of grief. There were so many questions I wanted to ask her, and experiences I longed to share with her. She had always longed to be a grandmother and had even made toys for her future grandchildren while she was sick, and now I was a mum, and she wasn't there to enjoy it, and my kids missed out on an amazing Granny. But I took comfort in knowing how happy she would have been for me in the joy of motherhood.

As I mentioned in the last chapter, grief for my Mum has never really finished. She is still not there (of course) and so I still miss her. Grief can never be fully resolved because the absent loved one continues to be absent. Someone told me that when you experience a loss it is like a gash is cut in the landscape of your life. Small griefs cut small gashes, major ones carve great gullies. The hole never goes away, but over time plants begin to grow again, and new beauty comes. But it is never the beauty that was. The landscape is never restored to its former state. In the same way, my life is very different to what it would have been had Mum lived. My daughter is a mum now, and I am loving supporting her and my granddaughter as she navigates the transition to motherhood. Her experience is so different to mine. I am grateful that I can be the Granny that Mum never got to be, but I am sad that both Mum and I missed out on so much because she couldn't be there for me.

As Christians we still grieve. Even when we know that the one we love is in heaven with God, and that we will see them again, we still miss having them here. There is nothing wrong with that. But we grieve *with* God. He promises to comfort us, and He is to be trusted. God in Jesus knows the reality of grief and understands our pain. We can safely express all our different emotions to Him.

———————— DIAMOND ————————

Grief is a part of life. When we grieve with God, He comforts us.

Clarity
From the Word – A truth to stand on
Brothers and sisters, we do not want you to be uninformed about those who sleep in death, so that you do not grieve like the rest of mankind, who have no hope. For we believe that Jesus died and rose again, and so we believe that God will bring with Jesus those who have fallen asleep in Him. 1 Thessalonians 4:13-14

Blessed are those who mourn, for they will be comforted. Matthew 5:4

Cut
What do you fear most about grief? Are there any feelings that you think you shouldn't bring to God? Ask Him what He thinks about that.

Colour
For your journal: Ask God to show you ways that He has comforted you in the past.

Carat
Declaration: We do not have to grieve as those who have no hope. Instead, we can grieve in God's arms, and allow Him to comfort us.

Chapter 13

What a Year

My husband Rob and I were thirty-one, with a one-year-old and a three-year-old, when he started to get weird pain in his left arm when he exercised. The pain was bad enough to send him to the doctor, but she wasn't concerned. He was young and healthy and had no risk factors for heart disease. To be on the safe side, though, she sent him for some tests. The results shocked everyone. She made frantic calls to the heart specialist and told me to make sure I knew the quickest way to the nearest hospital, while telling us not to panic and instructing Rob not to elevate his heart rate! It was very frightening. Rob had blocked coronary arteries. This was in 1994, and medicine was not as advanced as it is now, so Rob ended up spending a fair bit of time in the coronary ward, and having three procedures, which all ended up being unsuccessful. We said our farewells several times, as we weren't sure how long he would live. During the months when this was going on, I managed to accidentally get pregnant twice (worry made us careless). Even though it wasn't planned I was thrilled as I desperately wanted a third child, and it seemed a sign of hope in the middle of everything that was going on. Both pregnancies ended in miscarriage.

The first one was so hard. We had gone away for a weekend to recover from the second procedure and to regroup a little. We were hopeful that this time Rob's problem would be fixed. While we were away I started bleeding, so we came home early so I could rest. Meantime, Rob thought it would be a good idea to climb a ladder in the rain to clear the gutters. The ladder slipped on the wet ground, and he fell on a railway sleeper edging the garden, breaking several ribs. I rushed him to emergency. They weren't too concerned until we mentioned that they had recently inserted a stent into a coronary artery, and he was on blood thinners. He suddenly became very interesting indeed. I stupidly mentioned my bleeding, so they insisted on examining me as well. I ended up on a gurney at two in the morning watching Rob being wheeled away to be transferred by ambulance to another hospital while a doctor with no bed side manner examined me and asked why on earth I was crying. When the nurse explained he graciously gave me permission to cry!

I ended up miscarrying the next day, while Rob was still in another hospital. It was just awful. I felt so frustrated with God. I didn't seek this pregnancy and yet it had seemed such a blessing. Why had he allowed me to get pregnant only to take it away again? It seemed such a waste of grief.

The second pregnancy lasted longer but was a bit easier as I protected my heart more and didn't commit as strongly to this new baby. I tried not to imagine a future with three kids. By ten weeks I was starting to get hopeful though, but then all my hopes came crashing down. Meanwhile, Rob's symptoms were back, so he was back in hospital for more surgery. I started to feel embarrassed asking for prayer – we seemed to be demanding too much attention!

That same year there were other stressors as well. A dear friend ended up in ICU for a month with his life in the balance (he fully recovered), my aunt had a brain aneurism and barely survived surgery, and then my uncle was diagnosed with liver cancer and died three months later aged 45. I got to the point that I didn't want to answer to phone as it always seemed to bring bad news.

I became numb and it felt like there were no emotions left. I continued to trust God but I didn't think that He knew how much I could bear. I became afraid that I would be broken by all this. It felt like the world was a hostile place.

Again and again I was confronted with the choice – to turn away from God or lean into Him. He gave me grace in spite of my pain, and I leant in. God began to sprinkle signs of hope in my path, and life became easier. We thought that Rob would need bypass surgery as the simpler procedures had failed, but they decided to try to manage his condition with medication instead, and it worked. This was great news, as at that time a bypass only tended to last for ten years, so we were looking at a lot of operations! We had been looking for ways to move back to Brisbane to be near family, and a way opened up to our great joy. I became pregnant again, and God blessed us with our wonderful son Stephen. The rush of bad news subsided, and joy returned.

I often wonder why we had that terrible year. I don't believe God sent it. God is the giver of good gifts. But God certainly used it. Again, He showed me that no matter what happened He would always be there, and that my faith would survive whatever Satan threw at it. It didn't ultimately weaken my faith. Instead, it strengthened it. It confirmed that my faith wasn't based on being blessed by God – that I could praise Him no matter what happened.

DIAMOND

Being a Christian doesn't mean that bad things don't happen to us. It does mean that we can trust God to be with us whatever happens.

Clarity
From the Word – A truth to stand on
I know what it is to be in need, and I know what it is to have plenty. I have learned the secret of being content in any and every situation, whether well fed or hungry, whether living in plenty or in want. I can do all this through Him who gives me strength.
Philippians 4:12-13

"I have told you these things, so that in me you may have peace. In this world you will have trouble. But take heart! I have overcome the world."
John 16:33

Cut
How do you feel when you read all the passages in the Bible talking about how we will suffer? How does suffering fit in with your understanding of God?

Colour
For your journal: Ask God to show you how He can be faithful even when you suffer, or to remind you of His faithfulness in the past when you have endured suffering.

Carat
Declaration: Even when bad things happen to me and I suffer I can trust that God is good and will always be with me.

Chapter 14

Cancer?

It had been a week of tests, trying to determine why I was so tired. I had half expected the doctor to dismiss my concerns – what working mother of three teenagers isn't tired – but she was determined to get to the bottom of things. After some strange blood test results, I was sent to have an abdominal ultrasound. All seemed ok until the radiographer got to the left kidney. 'I'll need to call your doctor – you need a contrast CT scan', he said. 'Actually, I'm just going to do it. It needs to be done NOW.'

I tried not to panic as I was escorted to another room, telling myself it was probably just caution, but as I lay there going in and out of the noisy machine it was hard not to think of worst-case scenarios. I was 46 – just 3 months off the age at which my mother had died of cancer. I knew that I was not invincible.

As it was late in the afternoon, they were able to give me the scans but not the doctor's report. I was told to make an appointment with my doctor the following day where I would receive the results.

'What about the cost?' I asked.

'Oh, don't worry, we won't charge you a fee today,' they said.

The waiving of the fee spoke volumes. I had been quoted a reasonably large fee just for the ultrasound, and they had done a CT scan as well. This was obviously something serious.

As I sat and waited for the scans to be ready, I told myself to just breathe, that it would be ok, whatever the result. God would be there. It was funny, but there was a sense of familiarity, of having done this before. Then I realised that it was like all the times I had done something I feared – like jumping off the ledge in a high-ropes course or abseiling off a cliff – when I needed to be brave and do something that I knew was safe but that looked anything but. I was glad that I had practiced bravery as I needed to be brave now.

The thought of waiting nearly a whole day to find out what was wrong seemed unbearable. Fortunately, my uncle is a radiologist, and he lives nearby, so I rang him to see if he would be able to look at the scans. Poor James: he had had to walk the cancer journey with his sister (my mum), and now he had to tell her daughter bad news. It was a large tumor in my kidney, most likely cancerous, and it seemed that there was lymphatic involvement, as the lymph glands were all enlarged. He told me that if it was contained in the kidney then the outlook was very good, and that there wasn't a chemotherapy for kidney cancer, so whatever happened I wouldn't have to face that. He didn't want to talk about what would happen if it was in the lymph nodes, and I decided I wouldn't go there either at this stage. I had enough to think about.

I don't remember the phone call to tell my husband and my father. I remember that we decided that we wouldn't tell the kids until the next day, when we had come to terms with it a little. I remember going to get my daughter from ballet on my way home and feeling totally surreal. God gave us the strength to be with our kids that night, but it was a relief to retreat to our room and to start to come to terms with a life turned upside down.

That night we made some decisions. We would choose hope over negativity whenever possible, but we would also face the facts. We would not hide anything from the kids. I had seen firsthand the pain caused by different things being told to different people. They were part of this journey, and I wasn't going to lie to them. But we would present as hopeful a message as we could.

As I lay in bed that night, I felt a strange joy. In spite of everything, God was with me. Whatever happened, I knew that He had me in His hands. I remembered Romans 12:1 *'Therefore I urge you, brothers and sisters, in view of God's mercy, to offer your bodies as a living sacrifice, holy and pleasing to God – this is your true and proper worship.'* I didn't feel I needed to ask for healing, I just wanted to focus on God. I offered my body to Him, to do with as He willed – to heal or not to heal, to give life or take me home to Him. I told him my heart's desire was to see my children's children grown, but I left it in His hands. He gave me such peace, peace that passes understanding. In my time of need His grace was sufficient for me, just as He had promised.

The next day was a whirl, as we visited the local doctor and the kidney specialist who would treat me. He ordered further scans, but planned surgery for the following week.

Our next task was telling the kids. Jessica was the hardest. She was nearly 17 at the time, in the middle of her final year of high school, and a week off sitting major exams. Not an ideal time for me to be sick. When I told her that it looked like I probably had cancer, her response was so hard to hear.

'Are you going to die like your mum?' I swallowed hard and told her we really didn't know, but we hoped not.

'Am I going to die when I am 47?' This question knocked me for six, but I reassured her as best I could.

'How will I cope if you die?' At least I had an answer for that one. I asked her if she saw me as a broken person.

'No Mum, you're amazing,' she said.

I told her what she already knew. That losing my mum was the hardest thing I had ever faced, and that I was still sad that she wasn't alive, that I missed her all the time. But that God had given me great blessings through my mum's illness and death. That He had cared for me, and sent people to help me, and had taught me how to help others going through hard times. That He had strengthened my faith and my character. I was able to reassure my beautiful Jess that while she would always be sad if I died, that it wouldn't destroy her, that help would be given if she reached out for it, and that it would only make her a more beautiful, loving and faith-filled person if she put her trust in God. I was so grateful that I was able to reassure us both.

The rest of the week before the surgery is a bit of a blur. I was trying to get everything organised before I was out of action for eight weeks and to tell everyone who needed to know what was going on. But amidst the busyness and the emotion – mine and everyone else's – the amazing peace and joy continued. I was in God's hands, and He helped me to keep my eyes on Him, not on my circumstances.

I was overwhelmed by the outpouring of love that I received as the news spread. So many messages from people telling me what I meant to them and the impact that my life had had on them. It was incredibly reassuring. Before this I had had some fears that I had wasted my life, choosing to focus on family and community rather than career when I had been very academically successful in my youth. Now I knew that if it was my time to die I had no real regrets. I had invested my time in the people that mattered most to me, and so many were telling me that my life was significant, that I had made a difference to them.

The hardest time was the night before the surgery. I had planned a nice roast dinner with the immediate family, but first my husband Rob and I had to have a final doctor's visit to confirm everything before the operation the next day. The doctor started talking about life with one kidney – the things I needed to do to keep healthy post-surgery. Then he looked at the scans I had had done the previous day. His face changed.

'I think I shouldn't operate after all,' he said. 'The lymph nodes look bad. If the cancer is in the lymph nodes, you have a very limited life expectancy – probably just a couple of months. I'm not sure if it's wise to spend those months recovering from a major surgery like this.'

It was so hard to hear, but we had to make a decision then and there about what to do. Rob and I looked at each other, and both said that we wanted to go ahead with the surgery. The doctor hummed and ha-ed a bit and then agreed to operate as planned. We decided not to say anything about this to the kids, as there would be time enough when we knew for certain.

That was a strange evening. I was trying to be cheerful for the kids, but there was this new sense of uncertainty hanging over me. So many people rang to wish me well, which was lovely but exhausting, particularly as I was trying to stay upbeat, and Jess had a chemistry assignment that she wanted my help with, so I was trying to do that. Finally, it was time to go to bed ready for the morrow. Rob and I committed it all to God yet again.

My calm deserted me a bit as I was waiting for the surgery in the morning. My operation was delayed, and the long period in the waiting room with all these people having minor surgeries was hard to bear. I ended up in tears waiting on the gurney for my surgery to start, and the lovely anesthetist took the time to sit with me and hold my hand as we waited for it to be time for me to be put under.

After surgery, the news was good. First, amazingly, the lymph nodes were indeed enlarged, but they were full of fatty tissue - not cancer! That meant that I didn't have stage four kidney cancer after all. Then after a few days we received even better news. I had a rare benign tumor. In some cases they are pre-cancerous, but in my case it was completely benign. To me it was a miracle. I wasn't going to die around my 47th

birthday like my mum, and I could hope to see my grandchildren born and grown up. The doctor thought that the extreme tiredness and unwellness I was experiencing, which took me to the doctor in the first place, must be caused by something else, as my sort of tumor is normally asymptomatic, but as I recovered from the surgery my normal health returned. I can't prove that God healed me of stage four kidney cancer, but it sure felt like it to me.

As I began to recover after the surgery, I faced a fresh challenge. I had grieved long and hard for my mum as I matured and became a mother myself, focusing on what I had lost. Now I was confronted with her loss in a new way. I mourned for her situation – a youngish woman having to farewell her husband and four children, seeing her body deteriorate and losing her dreams of adventures and grandchildren and seeing her children grown up. It could so easily have been me too. I wept for my mum and ended up seeing a counsellor to help me process all the different feelings. It was healing though. I finally felt that I could let her go; that after twenty-two years, my grief work was completed, though of course sadness still remained.

It was amazing to see how God used my situation in many different ways. It quickly bore fruit in Jess' life, in a way that we wouldn't have chosen. Just a few months later the mother of one of her close friends committed suicide. She didn't want to talk to any of her friends but felt able to talk to Jess because she knew that Jess had feared losing her mum. It was helpful on a practical level, too, as Jess knew the things that needed to be done to apply for special consideration at school.

For me, the depth of love and peace that God showed me in the middle of trial was so strengthening. I felt a little like Shadrack, Meshack and Abednego who said that they knew that God could save them, and that He would, but that even if He didn't they would not bow down to Nebuchadnezzar's statue (Daniel 3:16-18). I knew that God could save me, but far more important than healing was that He loved me and was with me.

Growing up, I thought that God wanted us to suppress our desires, that He wanted me to be less so that He could be more. I see now that I misunderstood Him. My desire for health and a long life were not wrong, and God wanted me to tell Him about it, but I think if I had clung too tightly to that desire I would have lost some of the joy that God wanted to give me. More than healing, He wanted to give me Himself.

It's easy for me to forget this lesson in lesser trials. When the big things hit us, we know that we need to lean on God and ask for Him to help us to trust Him. But I find that in the day to day trials I tend to focus on what I need God to do to fix things for me, rather than clinging to Him. It has been good for me to be reminded of this as I write this. For He is God and I am not, and God is better than any gift He could give me.

DIAMOND

While God loves to bless us with good gifts,
His greatest blessing is Himself.

Clarity
From the Word – A truth to stand on
Shadrach, Meshach and Abednego replied to him, "King Nebuchadnezzar, we do not need to defend ourselves before you in this matter. If we are thrown into the blazing furnace, the God we serve is able to deliver us from it, and he will deliver us from Your Majesty's hand. But even if he does not, we want you to know, Your Majesty, that we will not serve your gods or worship the image of gold you have set up." Daniel 3:16-18

Cut
Ask God to show you if you are focusing more on what He can do for you than on who He is. Sit before Him with open hands, releasing the things you've been holding on to so tightly, and receive Him in return.

Colour
For your journal: Set aside some time to sit with God and open your heart to Him. Write down all the things you desire, big and small. Then ask God to show Himself to you, in the middle of your desires.

Carat
Declaration: God, You are the best gift there is. Forgive me for focusing more on Your gifts than on You, the giver. Thankyou that You love to bless me, and that You will be with me whatever happens.

Chapter 15

Strength in Weakness

But He said to me, 'My grace is sufficient for you, for my power is made perfect in weakness.' Therefore, I will boast all the more gladly about my weaknesses, so that Christ's power may rest on me. That is why, for Christ's sake, I delight in weaknesses, in insults, in hardships, in persecutions, in difficulties. For when I am weak, then I am strong.
—2 Corinthians 12:9-10

I have a bit of a love/hate relationship with these verses. In one way it is encouraging. I can trust God to use me in my weakness. But I hate feeling weak. I like to feel strong, competent, in control. I don't like to feel needy or dependent. But that is the reality. I can't even control the cells of my body. As Jesus said, I can't add even one day to the length of my life. I AM dependent. Refusing to acknowledge that does not make me less dependent, it just makes me more able to be deceived.

I realised that when I feel strong and in control I am believing a lie about myself. The very first part of the armor of God in Ephesians 6:14 is the belt of truth. Truth is the foundation on which the armor is built.

We need to build on truth, not lies. If I think that I can stand alone and do what God has called me to do in my own strength I am building my armor onto a lie, and I am exposed to risk. I open the door to pride and competition and fear. When I acknowledge, truly acknowledge, that I can do nothing in my own strength then I am released to do what God is calling me to do in his strength.

As God taught me about this, He reminded me of being a little girl with my Daddy. I saw my little hands in Daddy's big hands, 'building' with a hammer and saw. I saw myself sitting on my Daddy's knee and 'driving' our car down the long driveway on our property. I remember dancing with my little feet on Daddy's big feet, my little hands in his big, strong hands, feeling like a princess. His hands were so gentle, and yet so strong. I was safe doing things that I couldn't do, because I was doing them with my Daddy.

Pretending to be strong is hard work. It means that I have to hide my need, that I have to keep other people away or they might see through the façade. Knowing that the strength is not mine but God's is incredibly freeing. It doesn't mean that I don't do the work. It isn't an excuse for poor preparation, or lack of planning. It means that I acknowledge truth in my heart – that I am like a little child, and that my Daddy is guiding me and enabling me in all that I do, so I don't need to be afraid.

God is the one who is strong. We are weak, and when we acknowledge that and lean into His strength then we become strong in Him.

Clarity
From the Word – A truth to stand on
But He said to me, "My grace is sufficient for you, for my power is made perfect in weakness." Therefore I will boast all the more gladly about my weaknesses, so that Christ's power may rest on me. 2 Corinthians 12:9

Cut
How does acknowledging your weakness and dependence make you feel? What areas of weakness do you find the most difficult?

Colour
For your journal: Ask God to show you a time when He has made His power perfect through your weakness. What did you learn about the beauty of your weakness and His strength?

Carat
Declaration: God is strong, I am weak. I am dependent on God for everything. I can rejoice in this and boast in His strength. For when I am weak, I am strong.

SECTION

4

When God Does the Unexpected

Chapter 16

An Encounter with Holy Spirit

Some experiences are just so hard to put into words. How do you describe the first days of a new love without sounding ridiculous? How do you describe a sunset, or the way you felt when you received good news? Experiences with God can be like that, only more so. If we can't find words to adequately describe something as simple as a sunset, how can we possibly find adequate words for God, or for the way that He works in us? So, remembering that words are but poor substitutes for reality, let me try to describe how God touched me a few years ago.

For most of my life I have struggled to feel God's love. As I've already discussed, at perhaps tedious length, I believed lies about Him and thought I had to earn His love. I also felt overlooked by Him. Other people seemed to have amazing experiences with Him, where He spoke to them or touched them in special ways, but it never seemed to happen to me. I felt like one who watched, while others experienced.

Holy Spirit had always intrigued and yet frightened me. I was a teenager during the Charismatic Renewal, when the church seemed to rediscover the Holy Spirit and His gifts. People spoke in tongues and prayed for miracles. God seemed to act and speak in extraordinary ways. What I saw made me long for a closer relationship with God, but it also put me off. It seemed to me that in order to walk with God in that way I had to leave my mind behind. It seemed to be based on emotion. I also saw what seemed to me a lot of manipulation and misrepresentation. I felt like I had to pretend to be something I wasn't in order to experience God in this way.

Over the years my husband and I had various friends who knew God like this, and they blessed us, but I stayed away in fear of being misled. Finally, I came to a church where I was taught by people who used their minds clearly - they were logical, well-educated and analytical - but they also spoke in tongues and saw miracles and heard God's voice. Little by little, I began to hope that maybe God was still active today in the ways I saw in the Bible. I started to expose myself to places where I saw the Holy Spirit moving, going to conferences, reading books, getting involved with what was happening at our church. At first, I was quite judgmental, but slowly I was convinced that it was God working. But still none of it happened to me. I saw my friends and people I respected being overwhelmed by the Spirit – shaking, crying, laughing, falling down – and I saw evidence of change in their lives, enough to convince me that it really was God. But even though I was prayed for and went down the front and asked God to touch me, I still seemed to be left out.

The one thing I really didn't want to happen to me was laughter. I couldn't understand how laughter could be a response to God's presence, and I hated the thought of looking so ridiculous. Laughing didn't seem to accord with the dignity of God. I was unsure too, about all the shaking that seemed to go on. I wanted God to touch me, but in a nice, calm, sensible way.

At the end of a conference at our church, the speaker prayed for me, and I fell down in the Spirit and my hand shook a little. I was very moved, and happy that finally God had noticed me. Later that week I was lying in bed going to sleep when my hand started to shake again, and then I started to laugh. I laughed very loudly and uncontrollably for an hour! My poor husband couldn't work out what was going on. For me it was a beautiful blessing. I knew that I hadn't been manipulated by anyone, because no-one was there, and it wasn't embarrassing because it wasn't in public. I was happy. I had had a nice little controlled experience with God, and now I could relax.

I couldn't have been more wrong. That weekend we went on a church Encounter weekend, where we made space for God to move. Things often became quite noisy and chaotic on these weekends, and lives were changed. I was supposed to be on the prayer team. That Saturday, my nice, private, controlled little experience became a noisy, uncontrolled, public experience. I spent the weekend shaking, laughing and falling over, to the point where someone who didn't know me thought that I had Parkinson's disease. I had to have someone cut up my food and carry my plate as I could barely stand. It was overwhelming, embarrassing and exhausting. However, I absolutely knew that it was God, because I was filled with a desire to worship Him, and I started to experience His love in a way I never had before.

The next months were a rollercoaster. I lost 2kg in the first two weeks, as I was shaking so much, and was hungrier for God than for food. God woke me every night to talk to me and revealed things I couldn't have known. Not that He spoke in an audible voice, but as I prayed I sensed His still, small voice in my heart. Often, I would write what I thought He was saying in my journal. They didn't feel like my words – the way of thinking was so different from mine, and I was so blessed by what I heard Him saying. I spent hours every day worshipping Him, not as a task but as a thirsty person drinks water. I read chapter after chapter of the Bible, as it suddenly came alive in a new way. For the first few weeks I spent almost every moment possible fully focused on God. I didn't read a book other than the Bible, or watch TV, or listen to the radio. It was a time set apart.

A couple of days into this time, God asked me a question. I was worshipping Him in the middle of the night, and suddenly there was a stillness. I stopped shaking, and it was like the world went quiet. God asked me if I accepted what He was doing. He told me that I had a choice as to whether this would continue or not. He said that He had chosen me, and that there would be great joy, but there would also be a price to pay. He didn't tell me the price, but He asked me if I would pay it. It felt like heaven and earth stopped to wait for my answer. I thought about it, and then said yes. I felt a sense of celebration all around me, as that deep quietness passed. I didn't know what I had said yes to, but I knew that I had said yes to God long ago and I wasn't going to stop now. When the shaking and laughing started I had said to God that whatever it cost me, I would not ask Him to stop it, so it was really just a confirmation of that. (I did ask Him not to make me laugh out loud in church as I didn't want to distract people).

Someone gave me the verse from 2 Samuel 6:22 where David said when his wife criticised him for his unrestrained dancing: *"I will become even more undignified than this, and I will be humiliated in my own eyes."* I felt like God was telling me not to worry about what people thought, but to keep my eyes on Him. It hasn't been easy, and it has often been inconvenient, but God has blessed me so much.

Early on in this period, I asked God which member of the Trinity was speaking to me. He quickly answered it was the Holy Spirit, but that I could call Him Fred. I was horrified, and sure that I couldn't be hearing right. However, God had been talking to me about names, and their meanings, so I asked Him if it was short for Fredrick. He laughed, and said, no, it was short for Freedom. He explained that He knew that it was hard for me to relate to the Holy Spirt as a person rather than a force, and so He told me I could call Him Fred so that I could relate to

Him more easily. It was incredibly kind and made it so much easier for me to get to know this person of the Trinity. (Note that He didn't say His name was Fred, just that that was what I could call Him).

Over the following months God continued to speak to me daily. I didn't have a full night's sleep for more than three months, and I continued to be shaken on and off for years. My view of myself and God was radically changed, as I experienced Him more and more deeply. I discovered for myself the truth of Romans 8:15-16

'The Spirit you received does not make you slaves, so that you live in fear again; rather, the Spirit you received brought about your adoption to sonship. And by Him we cry, 'Abba, Father.' The Spirit himself testifies with our spirit that we are God's children.'

It became natural for me to call God 'Daddy', and to receive His love as His little child. It became natural for me to expect to hear God speak to me, and to use me to bless others. It awakened gifts I didn't know I had and lifted so much fear off me. I think that part of the reason that God needed to speak to me through my body was that I was so used to relating to Him just through my mind. This period was a real reset for me.

It has now been nine years since this encounter began, and the intensity has faded. But the experience forever changed me. It changed how I saw God and how I saw myself. It gave me courage to leave my job and go to Bible college, and then vocational ministry. It gave me courage to preach - and to write a book! Many of the diamonds that I share in this book were forged from this experience. It was embarrassing and awkward, tiring and costly, but so full of joy and love.

As you read this, you may long for an experience like this with God. I would encourage you to ask Him. But don't expect Him to relate to you in the same way that He related to me. He is a person of infinite variety. Open yourself to Him and trust Him, and He will meet you the way that you need to be met.

———————— DIAMOND ————————

We need Holy Spirit to empower us in our relationship with God. He is a person of infinite variety, and we will probably be surprised by how He works in us.

Clarity
From the Word – A truth to stand on
The wind blows wherever it pleases. You hear its sound, but you cannot tell where it comes from or where it is going. So it is with everyone born of the Spirit. John 3:8

Cut
How did the description of my encounter with God affect you? Did you feel jealous, excited, critical, happy, wistful? How do you feel about God doing things you don't understand? Ask God to show you if you are limiting the ways He can interact with you.

Colour
For your journal: Take your feelings to God. Ask Him to reveal Himself to you in new ways. Tell Him your fears and your longings.

Carat
Declaration: God, I submit myself to You. I remove any limits I have set on how I relate to You. You are trustworthy, and I put myself in Your hands.

Chapter 17

Disappointment

After the experience I described in *Encounter* life with God seemed so exciting. I was hungry for Him and He was present wherever I looked. Nothing was more satisfying than spending hours just worshiping Him. I saw miracles happen and filled journal after journal with what I heard Him saying to me. Life was made new. I thought that this was my new normal, and I was so happy. I felt that He was preparing me for a new way of serving Him. Everything seemed to point towards vocational ministry. I was scared but excited. I had been working as a school chaplain for years, but I felt God wanted me to leave that and study towards a degree in theology.

The months leading up to starting my degree were incredibly difficult. I had emergency surgery for some tumors that were blocking my small bowel. It was hard to hear another cancer diagnosis, though this time the medical prognosis was good. My recovery period was slow and difficult, with lots of pain, nausea and weakness. It was hard because it happened four weeks before I finished up my job as a chaplain, so I wasn't able to say goodbye as I had hoped. The day after my surgery my uncle underwent major surgery for bowel cancer, which unfortunately was unsuccessful, and he died a couple of agonising months later. Then my father-in law was diagnosed with stage four melanoma. He failed quite quickly, and we brought him home to our place for palliative care. I was the main carer, so I had the privilege of nursing him in his last days. He died in my home two days before study started! Even though all this was emotionally exhausting I was still filled with hope. God was with me, and He was preparing me for this new field of ministry.

But things didn't work out as I expected. The job that I thought God was preparing me for was given to someone else. Other doors closed. There were some exciting opportunities to preach and to minister to people, but they didn't seem to lead to anything. I felt like I was in a holding pattern. It was hard not to be disappointed with God. Why had He called me out of a job that I loved only to leave me apparently forgotten?

As I processed this, my closeness with God slipped away, and my joy was replaced with frustration. Spending time with Him became harder, as I had so many questions. It was tempting to reject my earlier experience, but I couldn't. I knew that God had truly touched me, and I knew that whatever happened I would never stop serving Him. But it didn't make the pain or the questions go away. I felt hopeless and abandoned, wondering why God hadn't just left me as I was.

Is this how David felt, when he was pretending to be mad in the court of the Philistines or running from his king in the desert (1 Samuel)? After his dramatic anointing as king by Samuel, his amazing defeat of Goliath and the invitation to life at the palace, he must have wondered how it all went so wrong. Maybe he would have been better off staying a shepherd in his father's fields?

Or how Joseph felt sitting in jail? God seemed to have offered him so much, with his dreams of greatness, his multi-coloured coat, and his high position in Potiphar's household. Now he was apparently abandoned and forgotten. Where was God in all this (Genesis 37-40)?

Or how Sarai/ Sarah felt, hearing repeatedly how Abraham was going to be the father of nations, while she, his wife, faced fresh disappointment month after month. How difficult it must have been for her, torn between trying to come to a place of acceptance of infertility while also trying to trust in what God said. The older she got the more she must have wondered if God truly had spoken, or if she had failed in some way. It's not surprising that after waiting ten years she looked for her own way to make God's promise come true, telling Abraham to sleep with her slave in her place (Genesis 12-17), or that after twenty-four years she laughed when angels prophesied that she would bear a son (Genesis 18:9-15).

Or Esther, chosen from the crowd to be a queen, but forgotten by her husband and forced to risk her life to try to save her people (Esther).

Or Moses, protected as a baby from death, brought up in the palace, seemingly being prepared by God to lead his people, but forced to flee everything he had ever known and work as a shepherd among foreigners for forty years. At eighty, he must have felt that God had passed him by (Exodus 2-3).

Or the Jews, waiting for their promised Messiah who would overthrow the Romans and restore Israel to her former glory, only to receive a Messiah who took no interest in politics and warfare, who said that His Kingdom was not of this world. Even the disciples seemed to be expecting political leadership with seats for them on the king's right and left, and instead they got poverty and martyrdom.

Over and over again in the Bible we see God calling people out, making promises to them, only for them to face long seasons of trial and waiting, and often a fulfillment that was different from what they expected.

When I feel overwhelmed with disappointment, and it feels like God has failed me, I remember these heroes of the Bible. It is easy for us to skim over their waiting and to focus on the end of the story, knowing that ultimately God does what He says He will do. But they were people just like us, and the long waiting and trusting seems to have been a crucial part of their journey. God is God and I am not. I can't expect to understand God. As His creature and His daughter, my place is to trust, even when I don't feel like it. Ultimately His way is best.

What does this look like for me? When I feel disappointed because it feels like God hasn't done what I thought He was going to do and He hasn't used me the way I expected, it's easy for me to discount and dismiss what He **has** done. To reject the powerful ways that He has worked in my life, because they weren't what I thought He was going to do. To miss out on the joy that I could have experienced in the actual life that I have lived, because I keep waiting for this other life to start. When I heard God speak to me, I thought that these years would have seen me pastoring in a church, and preaching to lots of people. They haven't looked like that. I have been ministering and speaking, but not as I expected. Has God worked? Have people been touched? Have I grown and developed? Yes and yes and yes. So why am I disappointed? Why can't I enjoy the blessings that I have? I'm believing a lie – that God has to work the way that I expected for it to be valid.

Hope is highly commended in the Bible. But hope is risky. To hope is to risk disappointment. Sometimes it seems safer to hope for nothing, to close down and live a quiet life, risking nothing. But God calls us to hope. Ultimately, we have every reason for hope. We know how the story ends: Satan will be defeated. The time of tears, of suffering, of pain and loss will be over. Glory will be revealed in us (Romans 8:18). But how do we live now? We have a choice to make. Do we continue to trust God, regardless of past disappointments, of bitter pain, or do we reject Him? The thing is, that now, in our time on earth, is the time when we can show God that we trust Him. When we are in the new earth when all pain is gone, all doubt is impossible, when what we only see dimly is clearly before our eyes, we won't be able to give trust without proof.

Love that only trusts when there is absolute proof is a weak sort of love. A friend who only trusted your word when you could prove it would be no true friend. When all looks black, when we have stepped out in faith only to be disappointed, when all hope seems gone - that is our shining hour. Our chance to show God how truly we love Him; that we trust Him in spite of outward appearances.

In those times, we choose to put our faith in who God is, not in what He does for us. When we are disappointed that God has apparently failed to act in accordance with His promise, we have a choice. We can be offended, and withdraw from Him, or we can choose to worship, even though this is hard. Worshiping reminds us of His character and His love for us, even when we don't feel it.

This doesn't mean that we don't allow ourselves to feel our disappointment. Pretending that we don't feel something we feel doesn't help anyone. God is the ultimate realist. The foundation garment of our armor against the enemy is the belt of truth. Coming to our Father with the truth of how we feel, crying with Him and expressing our pain is part of the healing. But we do it with God, and we ask Him to show us the truth of who He is.

Most Christians will have experienced times like this. In some ways, it is the true test of our faith – to continue to hope, when all hope seems gone; to trust, even though we seem to have been betrayed. But like Peter in John 6:68 we say to Jesus *'Lord, to whom shall we go? You have the words of eternal life, and we have believed, and have come to know, that you are the Holy One of God.'* We know that there is nowhere else for us – we have given our hearts to the most high God, and we will choose to hope in Him.

DIAMOND

Hope in disappointment is powerful. We have the choice to trust God in spite of our circumstances.

Clarity
From the Word – A truth to stand on
'Though the fig tree does not bud, and there are no grapes on the vines, though the olive crop fails and the fields produce no food, though there are no sheep in the pen and no cattle in the stalls, yet I will rejoice in the LORD, I will be joyful in God my Saviour.' Habakkuk 3:17

Cut
How has God disappointed you? Have you used this as a reason to press into Him, or to pull away from Him? Are you offended by God? If so, take the time to repent and to ask God to renew your mind.

Colour
For your journal: Rewrite the verse above from Habakkuk in your own words, with the areas where God may disappoint you in place of Habukkuk's fears. Make this your prayer.

Carat
Declaration: God is God, not me. I will choose to trust in Him whatever happens, even if it feels like He is failing me. I release all offence I have against Him and others, and I choose to hope in Him.

Chapter 18

The Potter

In the middle of the time of disappointment discussed above, I remembered how much I had loved doing pottery when I was younger, particularly throwing pots on a wheel. I needed something positive to comfort my soul, so I booked into a session. It was wonderful. For me, throwing pots is quite a meditative experience because your whole self, mind and body, are focused on that piece of clay. You don't just form it with your hands – you lean your whole body in, putting steady, firm but gentle pressure on the clay so that it is molded the way that you want it. Particularly in the centering stage, the clay seems to have a mind of its own, wobbling and moving in your hands as you strive to center it on the wheel. If you let it go its own way, it becomes more and more uncentered as the spinning wheel moves it. To center it you need to resist it, press against it.

As I worked, I remembered that God tells us that He is the Potter and we are the clay. Suddenly I was comforted. God showed me that just as I was fully focused on the clay, cupping my hands around it, leaning my body in to shape it, He had His hands around me. His resistance of me was not out of hate or forgetfulness – He had a plan, and it needed this process to get me there. He was not at a distance. Just as I would be covered in mud as I worked the clay, so He was in the muck with me as He grew me – not keeping a safe distance or using a production line.

The most time-consuming part of throwing a pot is centering the clay. You make a nice ball of clay, and throw it onto the wheel, as close to the center as you can. But if you want to successfully make a pot, it needs to be perfectly centered on the wheel. A lump of clay is hard to center - you need movement. So you press the clay upwards so that it forms a cone, and then you press it down again. This process is repeated several times until the clay is well centered on the wheel. Only once this is done can you start to form the pot.

I suddenly realised how pointless this would feel to the clay if it had feelings. It is formed up into a cone and then pressed back down into the lump it started as. Then the same thing happens again. And again. Over and over, for no apparent reason, as far as the clay is concerned. It would feel like a cruel trick. But from the potter's point of view, something incredibly important is happening. The wobbly, lumpy clay is slowly being centered. The bumps are being smoothed, the misalignment is removed. Finally, the potter has something he can work with. Perfectly centered clay is easy to form into a pot. It moves easily in your hands, responsive to your touch. In contrast, badly centered clay is a nightmare. It spins out of control so easily, and as you work the wobble becomes more and more pronounced until the whole thing collapses.

God showed me that I am not a good judge of progress in my life. I don't know what He is aiming to make from me; I don't know the places that I am off-center. I need a Potter. A Potter who has the patience and the commitment to center me and form me. To be firm and gentle as He resists my natural inclinations and brings me into alignment with Him. In Hebrews 12:10-11, we are told that God disciplines those He loves. However, He is never harsh or uncaring.

This picture of the potter changed my perspective completely. Where I had felt forgotten, I now felt loved. Where I had felt badly treated, I instead saw formation. Where I had felt that life was meaningless, I instead saw purpose and intention.

DIAMOND

God is forming us into the beautiful creation He has
in mind, just as a potter forms clay into a pot.

Clarity
From the Word – A truth to stand on
Yet you, LORD, are our Father. We are the clay; you are the Potter; we are all the work of your hand. Isaiah 64:8

Cut
Is there an area of your life where it feels as though God is failing you? Where things you expected to happen are not happening? Talk to God about your feelings and ask Him if you need to repent for lack of trust in Him.

Colour
For your journal: Watch a video of someone centering clay on a wheel, or actually go and take a pottery class. As you watch, ask God to show you the way He is working in your life. Ask Him to let you feel His hands around you and choose to trust Him to direct your life in the right way. Submit to His will.

Carat
Declaration: Father, You are the Potter, I am the clay. I give my life to You anew. Please mold me and make me as You desire. I trust You. Thankyou that You never leave me, and that You are the master craftsman.

Chapter 19

Most Highly Favoured Lady

> *In the sixth month of Elizabeth's pregnancy, God sent the angel Gabriel to Nazareth, a town in Galilee, to a virgin pledged to be married to a man named Joseph, a descendant of David. The virgin's name was Mary. The angel went to her and said, 'Greetings, you who are highly favored! The Lord is with you.'*
> —Luke 1:26-28

Imagine being a teenage girl, just going about your business, when suddenly an angel appears to tell you that you are a favoured one, and that the Lord is with you! I expect that if that happened to me, I would assume that all my troubles would be over. And yet Mary's life as it is recorded in the Bible was anything but easy. It is not what I would expect a highly favoured life to be like. Thinking about her makes me wonder if my understanding of what God's blessing looks like is mistaken. So, I decided to dig into her life, and ask God to teach me.

Mary was told that she was favoured, and blessed, and that God was with her. She was told that her son would be great, called the son of God and that He would have the throne of David. (Read the whole story in Luke 1). I find it interesting that she assumed that the baby would be conceived right away, not that it was a prophesy for when she was married. But she accepted a pregnancy out of marriage without question, even though it carried the risk of disgrace and even death.

I wonder what she thought was going to happen? The angel said that the baby would sit on the throne of David. Did she have visions of a palace, of a warrior son like King David, come to drive the Romans away and establish Israel's place in the world again? When we read the prayer of praise that she proclaimed when she was with Elizabeth (Luke 1:46-56) I suspect that that was exactly what she expected.

As she progressed through her pregnancy with this miracle child, I wonder what dreams she dreamed. I doubt that they included a long road trip while big with child or a birth far away from her family with only a manger in which to lay her baby.

Many of us have a sense of promise or call on our lives. A dream that God seems to have placed in our heart, either in a dramatic way or in a quiet knowing. Somehow, we expect that if we are called by God that things will be plain sailing, and if they are not we have missed His call, or misunderstood him. Looking at the life of Mary, we can see that this is not so.

Her life was anything but easy. Getting pregnant before you were married was a disaster in her culture, even if your man stood by you. She would have been looked down upon and shamed. Her initial conversation with Joseph must have been awful. How do you tell your fiancé that you are pregnant when he knows that he is not the father? Her birth experience sounds like a nightmare. I remember being pregnant with my first child. I was afraid of what was to come, even though I had the best of medical care. I remember lying awake worrying that I didn't have enough bibs and nappies for my baby, even though there was a shop around the corner. I cannot imagine having to travel a long distance, and then being homeless when I got there. God sent angels and shepherds, but there is no mention of a midwife. Did this young woman have to labour all alone, with only her husband to help her? We're not told.

All the miraculous visitors after the birth must have been reassuring (Luke 2:8-20). God hadn't forgotten them. And the amazing prophecies in the temple when they took Jesus to be consecrated would have been a blessing and an encouragement. (Luke 2:21-40). But she was told that a sword would pierce her soul – not a prophesy I would like to receive as a new mum (Luke 2:35)! Then having the terrifying experience of fleeing in the night to protect your son from murder (Matthew 2:13-18) – how blessed did she feel then?

We don't know much about Jesus' growing up years, only that He was filled with wisdom and was strong, and the grace of God was upon Him (Luke 2:40). Sounds like the perfect child. I'm not so sure about his disappearing act at Jerusalem when He was 12 though. I lost my son for a couple of hours when he was 10, and that was terrifying. Poor Mary and Joseph lost Jesus for THREE DAYS! And He does not seem to have understood why they were so upset. Mary said to Him, '*Son, why have you treated us like this? Your father and I have been anxiously searching for you.*' Jesus just said, '*Why were you searching for me? Didn't you know I had to be in my Father's house?*' (Luke 2:48-49). Apparently even a perfect, sinless man is still a teenager!

When Jesus started his ministry, Mary seems to have been with Him and the disciples. They were all together at the wedding in Cana, when the wine ran out. Mary knew that Jesus could fix it (How was she so sure?) and asked Him to sort it out. Jesus was apparently unwilling but seems to have done it to please His mum (John 2:1-11).

Later though things were more strained. When Jesus spoke at His hometown of Nazareth He was rejected by the people, and at one point the family thought that Jesus had lost his mind and tried to take Him home. He wouldn't go to them (Mark 3:20-21). In John 7 we are told that his brothers did not believe in Him. It must have been a really hard time for Mary. She had all these promises and prophesies about Jesus, but she seems to have not really known if they were working out or not.

Whatever her doubts, Mary was there when Jesus was crucified, and Jesus spoke to her from the cross, ensuring that she would be looked after when He was gone. What a bitter-sweet moment that must have been.

We have no record of her seeing the resurrected Jesus, but she and Jesus' brothers were in the upper room with the disciples at Pentecost. Jesus' brothers became evangelists – James became the head of the church in Jerusalem, and James and Jude both wrote letters that are in the Bible. We don't know what happened to Mary after that, but when I read Luke I always like to think that she was one of the witnesses that he spoke to – his story of Jesus conception, birth and early life seem to be very much from her point of view.

So that is Mary. Chosen by God. Blessed, highly favoured. God is with her. Honoured across the centuries by the church. But if you were offered the choice, would you choose her life? Would you be prepared to suffer as she had to suffer?

It's easy to look at great Christians, and to wish to be like them. To wish that God had chosen us like that. But I think that mostly if you talk to people who have been powerfully touched by God, there has been a deep price involved.

As I have tried to step out in faith to follow God, it has often been difficult. I have questioned myself, because everything hasn't just fallen into place as I expected. But looking at Mary's life reassures me.

Having God's favour doesn't mean that life will be easy. It doesn't mean that things won't go wrong. It doesn't mean that we will understand everything. But it does mean that God will always be with us.

I doubt that Mary had any real idea of what she was letting herself in for when she said yes to God, but she knew God and she trusted Him. We are told she '*treasured up all these things and pondered on them in her heart'* (Luke 2:19). At times she was afraid it was all going wrong, but it seems she continued to trust God anyway.

Saying yes to Jesus means that we will be blessed and loved, but it doesn't mean that we won't suffer. Suffering is not a sign that we are on the wrong path, or that we have misunderstood (though it is not a sign that we are on the right path either!). We are told repeatedly in the Bible that we can expect times of suffering.

Things may not have turned out as Mary expected, but I am sure that in spite of the pain she would not have changed it. If she could have made Jesus into a military commander who ejected the Romans instead of the Saviour of the world, would she have done it? Aren't you glad she didn't!

I hope that you have dreams for your life that you feel are blessed by God. Maybe people have prophesied over you and have seen exciting things in your future. You may feel called by God to serve Him in an extraordinary way. It's so exciting to take the first steps to follow those dreams or take up the calling. But a true calling from God doesn't mean that there will be no obstacles, or no suffering.

As I have struggled in those times, there are two things I repeatedly hear from God. First, He asks me to trust Him. Second, He reminds me that He is God, and I am not. He is the Leader, I am the follower. He is the Teacher, I am the student. He is the Father, I am the child.

Following God is not easy. He never told us it would be easy. But He told us that He would always be with us, that He would never leave us or forsake us, and that He would do more for us than we could ever ask or imagine. We have to choose – do we believe Him or not?

———————— DIAMOND ————————

God's blessing does not always look like blessing to us at the time, but God knows what He is doing!

Clarity
From the Word – A truth to stand on
Who shall separate us from the love of Christ? Shall trouble or hardship or persecution or famine or nakedness or danger or sword? Romans 8:35

Cut
How do you feel reflecting on Mary's journey? Does it change how you see your own journey?

Colour
For your journal: Ask God to show you how He sees some of the difficult times of your life

Carat
Declaration: I choose to trust God with my life. He is God and I am not. He knows what He is doing, and He will not fail me.

SECTION 5

God in the Everyday

Chapter 20

Friends with God?

I've always liked the idea of spiritual disciplines - those methods we can follow that help us to get to know God better. Regular practices like prayer, fasting, reading the Bible, silence, and retreat. But they haven't always worked that well for me. If I do them, I am tempted to feel proud, and to believe that God owes me something. If I don't I feel guilty and want to hide from God.

I'll never forget an experience I had as a teenager with fasting. I had decided to fast, and to go to the bush to spend the day with God in nature. I felt very holy. I found a nice spot and settled down to have a special time with God. There was just one problem. There were insects everywhere. I felt like I was covered with flies and ants and mosquitos and gnats. It was so hard to focus on the Bible and prayer. I asked God to take them away, but He didn't. Eventually I gave up in disgust and went home and ate lunch. What was the point in fasting and praying if God wouldn't even control the insects? I felt very hard done by. I had done my part, but God had let the side down!

My other problem with spiritual disciplines is when I don't do them. Particularly when I don't have a 'quiet time'. I get into a vicious cycle where my prayers tend to consist of me telling Him how sorry I am that I haven't been praying or reading the Bible more, and I feel condemned. Now I know that this is not God, because He tells us in Romans 8:1 that there is no condemnation for those who are in Christ Jesus. But I still tend to get stuck in that feeling, and so my desire to be with God decreases, because who wants to be with someone who is mad with them? It can spiral into a very bad place.

One time, I was in a period like this with God where I felt like He was angry with me (even though my head knew this was a lie) and spending time with Him seemed like such a burden. Someone told me to read Job 13:15, which in the NIV says '*Though He slay me, yet will I hope in him; I will surely defend my ways to his face.*' But I read it in the GNT, which reads, '*I've lost all hope, so what if God kills me? I am going to state my case to him.*' I was a bit taken aback, but it was a comfort in a strange sort of way, because in that moment that was how I felt – that I had lost all hope in God, and He may as well just kill me. And reading it in His word gave me words to say it to Him. I cried and told Him how tired I was of trying to read the Bible and pray. How tired I was of trying and failing and feeling guilty and believing that God was angry with me. How I was angry with God for making me like this and seeming to fail in His promises. I was in a bad place, but also a good place because I was really talking to God. What He said to me surprised and comforted me. He told me to stop. To stop trying to read the Bible and pray. To stop making it a duty and a burden. I felt so loved! It was like I had been at a banquet table and was being told that I had to eat everything in front of me. That sense of MUST took away my appetite completely. Now being told that I didn't have to eat anything if I didn't want to renewed my appetite and suddenly I wanted to talk to God. God is so kind!

For me, the danger with disciplines is my temptation to make them into a law that I do to earn favour or avoid punishment, rather than doing them out of love for God. Rule-following brings blessings and curses, rewards and punishment, commendation and condemnation. But God is not calling us to follow rules. He is calling us to friendship.

Jesus invited us to a new way, a way of relationship. He said, *'I no longer call you servants, because a servant does not know his master's business. Instead, I have called you friends, for everything that I learned from my Father I have made known to you.'* (John 15:15). Friends don't need rules. They function out of knowledge of and love for one another. Servants and slaves need rules. Rules represent a minimum requirement. You keep the rules, and you are done. Nothing more is required. Friendship is a total commitment. *'Greater love has no one than this: to lay down one's life for one's friends. You are my friends if you do what I command'* (John 15:13-14). Friendship with God requires obedience, but not rules. It is more complex than that. Friendship with God means being guided by the Spirit, and the Spirit is like the wind – He blows where He wills (John 3:8). Paul spent a lot of time talking about why we need to live by grace, not law. He was so determined that Christians would not constrain themselves to keeping the Law because he wanted them to be led by the Spirit. The Law brings condemnation and guilt, as Paul demonstrated in Romans 7. But life in the Spirit brings freedom. Not freedom from obedience, but freedom to obey joyfully.

As I talked to God about spiritual disciplines, he reminded me of my marriage. My husband Rob and I have a practice that we follow. You could call it a discipline, I guess. Each morning we take it in turns to bring each other breakfast in bed. It is always so lovely when it's my turn to be served. But often, when it is my turn to get up first, I really don't want to. I would much prefer to stay in bed. But I almost always get up and make Rob a cup of tea and something special or something ordinary for breakfast, depending on my mood. Serving each other in this way is a practice that Rob and I follow to help to keep our marriage strong. But I don't do it so that Rob will love me. I am not afraid that if I roll over and tell him that I am too tired to do it today that he will leave me. Rob loves me whether I make him breakfast or not. Even so, doing this for each other is a blessing to our marriage. It is a way of communicating our love, and of keeping it strong.

Spiritual disciplines are not a way to earn God's love. Failing to do them is not necessarily a sign that I love God less. Like everything, there are seasons with disciplines, and times when we have more or less time or energy to give to them. But if I never want to spend time with God, or engage in any spiritual discipline, it is a warning flag that all is not well. It doesn't mean that God is angry with me, or that He doesn't love me anymore, but it does probably mean that I need to find out what is the problem between us.

It is strange how easily we forget what an incredible privilege we have, to be able to spend time with the most high God, and share with Him all the tiny details of our lives. Turning this privilege into an obligation to be met is a terrible shame. Because we are human, we need habits to help us to continue to spend time with God, but not because we are afraid.

There are many wonderful books describing spiritual disciplines. Reading about different ways of spending time with God can be incredibly helpful, particularly if your relationship with Him is feeling stale. Choosing to set aside time regularly to be alone with God is wise, as it is so easy for us to forget Him in our busy lives, just as it is important to set aside time to invest in any relationship that is important to us.

Spiritual disciplines like prayer, fasting, solitude, silence, meditation and so many others are a wonderful way to deepen our relationship with God. When we choose to do them, even though we don't want to, because we know God loves us and we love Him, then they are enriching and beautiful. But when we do them out of fear or obligation, they can become a barrier between us and God. We forget that we are invited to friendship with God, and that He wants us to enjoy His presence, not endure it.

DIAMOND

God doesn't want us to spend time with Him to earn His love. He invites us to be with Him because He loves us.

Clarity
From the Word – A truth to stand on
My beloved spoke and said to me, "Arise, my darling, my beautiful one, come with me." Song of Songs 2:10

Cut
How do spiritual disciplines work for you? If you do them, do you do them from fear or because you are loved? Ask God to show you if you are believing any lies about spiritual disciplines or practices.

Colour
For your journal: What spiritual disciplines are you currently using, if any? Talk to God about what spiritual disciplines would be helpful for you at this time. You may like to read a book describing different options.

Carat
Declaration: I have the incredible privilege of a relationship with the creator of the universe. I choose to spend time with Him even when I don't want to not because I am afraid of punishment but because I love Him and He loves me.

Chapter 21

The Radiance of God's Glory

*The Son is the radiance of God's glory and the
exact representation of His being
—Hebrews 1:3*

I was on a prayer retreat in the mountains, and we were told to read Hebrews 1. I didn't get past the first part of verse 3. 'The Son is the radiance of God's glory'. It felt like those words were filling my head, resounding in my heart. But what did it mean? How is the Son the radiance of God's glory? And what is God's glory anyway? The word glory is all through the Bible, but I felt that I had never really understood it.

I asked God what He meant when He said that Jesus is radiance. He asked me what radiance was. I replied that I guess it is light, the light that emanates from something. And then it hit me. The radiance of the sun is how we see what the sun is like. It is too distant and too hot for us to experience it directly. But through its radiance we can encounter the sun. Jesus is God's way of showing us who He is and what He is like. Jesus is God made accessible to us human beings. And He is not a pale likeness. He is the exact representation of His being. Jesus told us that when we see Him we see the Father (John 12:45).

Suddenly I understood the Trinity better. The Trinity is the idea that God is at the same time One and Three. This is a mystery that no one can really understand, which shouldn't surprise us. A God fully understood by His creatures would be suspect as being their creation! The mystery of God's nature should lead us to worship Him, acknowledging how far beyond us He is.

But this verse gave me a glimpse of the nature of the Trinity. The Father is like the sun – the source. Jesus is the radiance, the light, the way that we can see what the Father is like. But what about the Holy Spirit? As I prayed I felt that God said that the Holy Spirit is like the heat – the power that comes from the sun, the way that we can experience the sun in our bodies. The heat from the sun warms us, and brings life to this world. The Holy Spirit is the same. He is the way that we access God's power. He is the way that we experience God in our beings. He is God within us.

I find this a helpful analogy because it gives me a glimpse of how the three persons of the Trinity are all one and yet all different. You can't separate sunlight or the heat from the sun from the star itself. Each part is the sun. When you see light coming in the window you say, "the sun is coming in." When you feel cold and want to warm up, you go and sit in the sun. When you see the star of the sun rising in the east you say, "the sun is coming up." And yet each part is distinct and different. So it is with the Father, the Son and the Holy Spirit. Each Person is God, but each Person is unique, and has different roles and attributes.

Another helpful part of this analogy is that even though the light and heat proceed from the sun, and are produced by the sun, you cannot have a functioning sun that does not produce light and heat. In the same way, the Son and the Holy Spirit proceed from the Father, and yet all three have existed forever. There never was a time when there was only Father.

As I thought about the Trinity being like the sun God brought another memory to mind. I love to see the sunrise, particularly over the ocean. One day as I was walking along the beach, watching the sky lightening and being marked by glory, I realised it was almost time. I stopped to wait and watch for that first glimmer of sunlight over the horizon. And I thought how fortunate I was to stop in just the right place, where the sun was directly in front of me. As soon as I thought it I knew how ridiculous I was. Everywhere on the beach is the perfect place to watch the sunrise if you are standing on an eastern facing beach. The sun is always directly in front of you. No matter how many people are on the beach, each person would see the sun centered on them. It seems as if it is there just for you alone. This is a picture of the way that God is deeply present with each one of us, with each of us at the centre of His attention.

Of course, this analogy, like all analogies of God, is incomplete, as there is nothing on the earth that can fully represent what God is like, but I find it helpful, and maybe you will too.

The Trinity is a mystery, but it is a blessing to meditate on it. God three in one and one in three means that God is complete in Himself. He did not have to create us so that He would have something to love, for love is at the centre of His being. The three Persons of the Trinity love and glorify each other. God created because He is love, not in order to have something to love. God doesn't need us.

Even though God is sufficient in Himself He is continually reaching out to create, reconcile and restore the universe. The Trinity shows us that mission is at the heart of who God is. The Father begets the Son who collaborates with the Father to send the Spirit. We are invited into His love relationship and into His mission. Just as God loves to reach out to His creation, to draw it back to Himself, so we are called to reach out to draw people back to God.

Many of us have a 'favourite' member of the Trinity. You might like Jesus best, as He seems more accessible and friendly. Perhaps you find the Father easier to relate to, or maybe the Holy Spirit. As I have journeyed with God I have found it helpful to ask God to help me to relate to each person of the Trinity, as each one reveals different aspects of His nature. I have always loved coming to the Father, and of recent years I have loved to call Him Daddy and sit with Him as His beloved daughter. I often find it helpful to pray to Jesus when I feel weak or tempted, because *"we do not have a high priest who is unable to empathise with our weaknesses, but we have one who has been tempted in every way, just as we are—yet He did not sin."* (Hebrews 4:15). Jesus knows what it is to be human, and we don't have to be afraid to share our struggles with Him. I have learned to ask the Spirit's help more too. I love this verse; *"In the same way, the Spirit helps us in our weakness. We do not know what we ought to pray for, but the Spirit Himself intercedes for us through wordless groans."* (Romans 8:26). I find it such a comfort to be able to pray in tongues in the power of the Spirit, trusting Him to pray for me.

We will never be able to fully understand God. He is infinite and we will be learning more about Him for all eternity. It is easy to dismiss the concept of the Trinity as too hard or as irrelevant to our everyday life, but I have found meditating upon it brings me closer to God and increases my desire to worship Him.

———————— DIAMOND ————————

God is three in one, and He loves to relate to us in each of His persons.

Clarity
From the Word – A truth to stand on
When the Advocate comes, whom I will send to you from the Father—the Spirit of truth who goes out from the Father—He will testify about me. John 15:26

Cut
How do you respond to the idea that God is three in one? Do you relate more easily to Father, Son or Holy Spirit? Why?

Colour
For your journal: Read John chapters 14 to 17. Ask Holy Spirit to highlight some verses to you that will help you understand the Trinity better. Write them in your journal and meditate on them.

Carat
Declaration: God is Father, Son and Holy Spirit. He loves me and blesses me in each of His persons.

Chapter 22

Fear

Do not be anxious about anything, but in every situation, by prayer and petition, with thanksgiving, present your requests to God.
—*Philippians 4:6*

I don't know how many times we are told in the Bible not to be afraid, or not to worry or be anxious, but it is certainly a very frequent admonition. I always thought that worry was something natural and unavoidable. One day God convicted me that it wasn't a character flaw, it was disobedience. I was choosing to disregard God, and to believe lies about Him. When I felt worried or anxious, I needed to confess it and repent, not just shrug my shoulders and think that I couldn't help it.

I don't think that the command not to be anxious is referring to that rush of fear that you get when something goes wrong or you get bad news. The Greek verb Paul uses here, and that Jesus uses in Matthew 6:25, 28 and Luke 12:22, 26 is merimnate. The form that they use make it an instruction referring to an on-going activity, not a once-off event. I think they are telling us not to hold on to worry or rely on it to take care of us. Jesus is very pragmatic. He tells his listeners that worrying is useless. *"Which of you by being anxious can add a single hour to his span of life?"* (Matthew 6:27). He reassures them that God knows their needs and will take care of them. But Jesus wants their focus to be on God's Kingdom and His righteousness (Matthew 6:26-33).

When I am fearful, I am believing a lie. I am saying that I think that either God is not powerful, or He is not good, or He doesn't love me. Basically, I am saying that I don't trust God.

As I prayed about why I feared, God showed me that I was trusting fear to keep me safe. I believed that if I worried about something then I would think of all the things that could go wrong, and I could protect myself from them. I also thought that I needed fear as a motivator. I was relying on fear to give me the impetus to do the things that needed to be done. If I feared failure, I would do good preparation. If I feared pain, I would do the exercises to keep my back flexible. I believed that if I stopped fearing, then I would stop acting.

But if God is commanding me not to fear, then I do not need to worry in order to be able to plan something successfully. I should be able to find motivation to do things that need to be done without being fearful of the consequences of not doing them.

We can rely on fear for many things. It can get us out of things we don't want to do. Fear of punishment or detection can control our desire to do wrong. It can seem to keep us safe in dangerous situations. It can motivate us towards good actions. But it is based in a lie. And ultimately it will fail us and steal from us – steal our peace and our sleep and our health and our self-esteem and our relationships and leave us nothing but regrets.

God tells us that perfect love casts out fear (1 John 4:18). Jesus told His disciples, *'Peace I leave with you, my peace I give to you; not as the world gives do I give to you. Let not your heart be troubled, neither let it be afraid'* (John 14:27). Getting rid of fear is a process, which involves taking our eyes off what we fear and putting our eyes on who God is. It is helpful to ask Him to show us the role that fear is playing in our life, what we are relying on it for. Then we can repent of that and ask Him to fulfill that role.

I have hesitated to include this chapter, as I know that for many people anxiety is a mental health condition that is real and significant and cannot be willed or thought away. If you struggle with anxiety, please do not hear this as condemnation (or even if you don't struggle with anxiety – there is no condemnation for us!). Get professional help, take medication if it is needed. God provides these helps for us. Gather support around you to give you the strength that you need. But also ask God to show you his love in the midst of your anxiety.

I wish I could say that I no longer fear and that I simply trust God. Unfortunately, I am a long way from that. But seeing and naming the lies I have been believing is helping me to trust God more.

DIAMOND

God does not want us to fear. He wants us to
live in abundance, trusting Him.

Clarity
From the Word – A truth to stand on
So do not fear, for I am with you; do not be dismayed, for I am your God. I will strengthen you and help you; I will uphold you with my righteous right hand. Isaiah 41:10

Cut
What do you rely on fear to do for you? Are you trusting it when you should be trusting God? Ask God to show you lies you are believing about needing to fear.

Colour
For your journal: What would your life be like if you relied less on fear? What would you do if you knew that you did not need to be afraid?

Carat
Declaration: God tells me not to be afraid. I choose to trust Him to keep me safe, and to believe Him when He says He will uphold me and strengthen me.

Chapter 23

Leaving and Cleaving

That is why a man leaves his father and mother and is united to his wife, and they become one flesh
—*Genesis 2:24*

Yesterday afternoon a young man came and asked our permission to propose to our daughter. We had known that this was likely of course, but somehow, we were still not prepared. We gladly gave our consent, as he is a wonderful, godly young man whom our daughter adores. But still, I couldn't sleep last night.

I know that this is right, that it is time. That this is what I dreamed of for my little girl – a godly man to share her life with. And yet, I know that it will never be the same again. She will never be mine in the same way. I had a little weep for what is past, while looking ahead to the joys of the future.

We know about leaving and cleaving in terms of marriage. Of the necessity of letting go of the birth family in order to create a new family.

But as I reflect on this stage of my life, I see that leaving and cleaving is not just about marriage. It is a pattern of our lives.

Throughout our lives, we need to let go of the season that is past and grasp hold of the new season. Doing that well is one of the signs of a happy and productive life. Leaving a season in a way that recognises its value and mourns it appropriately before embracing the next season enriches us. We need to keep an open mind and heart to see the good in what is coming as well as what is gone.

I'll always remember when my youngest son finished preschool. I really loved being a preschool mum. I loved volunteering as a classroom helper, enjoying good fellowship with the other parents, cherishing the relaxed, happy environment with no homework and few fixed requirements. And leaving preschool meant that all my kids would be in school. I wouldn't be a young mum with kids at home anymore. That stage of my life was gone forever. I remember crying as I drove away from preschool that last time. I loved being a mum to little kids. I had relished it to the utmost. And part of moving on was acknowledging that loss. That there was a loss, and something to be mourned. But I couldn't stay in that place. If I did, I would miss out on the blessings of the next stage of my life. I had to mourn that which past, and then leave it, and cleave to that which was coming.

We see this pattern repeated over and over in our lives. Even if no tragedy comes to us, there is a cycle of losing and finding inherent in the nature of life. As we grow from baby to child to teenager to adult, then perhaps to marriage and parenthood to middle age and finally old age (if we are lucky) and death there are always things that we lose and things that we gain. To live life well we need to learn to appreciate what is passing but be able to leave it and cleave to the new thing while we have it. Living life regretting what is past, or straining towards what is to come is hollow, and leads to bitterness and disappointment. The way to joyful life is to live fully in the time that we are in.

There are two opposite temptations that Satan uses to spoil the present for us. One is to refuse to let go of the past. The other (which I discuss in the next section) is to wish away the present, longing for the future. Both are a mistake. The time that we have is now. Now is when we can serve God; now is when we are alive.

DIAMOND

Living life well means letting go of what is
past and embracing each new season.

Clarity
From the Word – A truth to stand on
To everything there is a season, and a time for every purpose under heaven: a time to be born and a time to die, a time to plant and a time to uproot. Ecclesiastes 3:1-2

Cut
Ask God to show you if you have tried to hold onto a season that is in the past. Spend time thanking Him for the gifts of that season and release it to Him. Ask Him to open your heart to the blessings of now.

Colour
For your journal: Ask God to remind you of a season you left well. What helped you to do that? How has leaving that season well blessed you?

Carat
Declaration: God has given me many different seasons in my life. I will enjoy the blessings and learn the lessons that each one has for me and be thankful.

Chapter 24

Love the One You're With

*Give thanks in all circumstances; for this is
God's will for you in Christ Jesus.*
—*1 Thessalonians 5:18*

As I held my new baby, I dreamt of what was to come. Of the day when he would crawl and walk and talk. I was so impatient for each new stage to arrive.

As I dragged my heavy body through another long, hot day, trying to care for two little kids while waiting for the new one to be born, it felt like that day would never come, that I would be pregnant forever.

As I tried to get a five-year-old to do his home reading and put his shoes on while the three-year-old wanted to tell me stories and the new baby needed a feed I felt overwhelmed. I didn't know how long I could manage. When would this end?

Later as I drove and drove and drove and drove, always watching the clock for when the next after school activity started or finished, and my afternoons were broken into half hour segments between trips, I longed for the day this busyness would end, when time stretched out again.

As I sat beside a learner driver, trying hard to stay calm and encouraging while fearing for my life, I counted how many hours of this I would have to survive before three children had their licenses. Oh, the blessed day as each one in turn finally passed.

And now the days of active motherhood are over. Those days of babies and sleepless nights are just a memory. There are no more school runs or afternoon activities to worry about. No more school lunches to make, no more driving lessons to give. They are grown and gone. Joyfully, fittingly. The house is quiet. My time is much more my own.

Did I wish those years away? There were times that I did. That I just endured the day or the hour, wishing it would pass. But there was another side as well.

As a young mum I read somewhere that in each stage of life you should look for what you could uniquely do in that stage, and then do it and enjoy it. When you had little ones who loved parks, enjoy the park. When you had primary schoolers who loved to be with mum, embrace opportunities for time together. When you had teenagers who wanted to discuss life the universe and everything, stop and engage with them. Look for opportunities to exalt in the stage you were in.

I certainly didn't do this perfectly, but I found it such a helpful concept. It gave me the impetus to indulge my little boy's love of public transport by buying a 3-hour ticket and catching a train and a tram and a bus, and having an adventure for the price of a few dollars. It reminded me to stop and enjoy cuddling my little baby, knowing that the season for this would be short. It gave me the energy to make everyday activities into adventures by occasionally turning a drive into a mystery tour (letting the kids decide left or right at each intersection) or a grocery shop into a treasure hunt (can you find three round green vegetables, or two tins with red pictures....). It helped me to treasure the chance to talk with my kids one-on-one as I taught them to drive. It encouraged my husband and me to put in the energy to have family holidays and camping trips and to prioritise making memories as a family.

This doesn't only apply to children, of course. Each part of life seems long while we are in it, but when we look back it seems to have passed so quickly. It's so easy to wish each stage away. To think that life will really start when we grow up, or get married, or buy a house, or get that job. It is particularly so in transition seasons, where we are waiting impatiently for a new opportunity to open up, and where we are seems so pointless. God sometimes seems to move so slowly. And yet there are things we can only do in the season we are in, that will be gone in the future. Part of living well is to find those things and do them.

As I look back over my life, it's those times when I was present in the moment without wishing it away that I most cherish. So often, the challenge of a season is also what gives it its greatest joy, if we stop to enjoy it.

As you think about the season you are in now, ask yourself what you will miss about it in the future. Consider whether there are ways that you can be more present or enjoy it more. Nothing lasts forever, and a time will come back when you look nostalgically back at this time as being part of 'the good old days'.

DIAMOND

Each season has its joys and frustrations. Enjoy now.

Clarity
From the Word – A truth to stand on
He has made everything beautiful in its time. He has also set eternity in the human heart; yet no one can fathom what God has done from beginning to end. I know that there is nothing better for people than to be happy and to do good while they live. Ecclesiastes 3:11-12

Cut
Are you missing out on your current season by wishing it away? What thoughts are leading you to do that?

Colour
For your journal: What can you uniquely do in this current season of your life, that you will not be able to do when this season passes? Write down at least three ideas, and plan how you will do them.

Carat
Declaration: This season of my life is precious, even though it is hard at times. I will treasure the gifts that God is giving me. I won't wish this season away.

Conclusion

Diamonds. Beautiful and faceted. My prayer is that as you have read about these things that God has done in my life, that you will start to see some diamonds in your life. So often hard times or challenges feel like something we just want to get through and forget. But that is not God's way. If we let Him, He can take the worst thing or the most insignificant thing and bring good from it. So, these are some of the diamonds that God has given to me, crafted by transforming pain and confusion and misunderstanding into precious truths.

But diamonds are not much use on their own. A bag of loose diamonds is only a work in progress. Diamonds need to be cut and polished and set.

We have an heirloom pendant that has been worn by brides in my family for generations. It contains forty-two diamonds of different sizes carefully set to make a beautiful whole. While each diamond is beautiful by itself they are so much more beautiful together.

For me, each of the diamonds I have shared in my book has been a massive blessing from God. But they have taken time and polishing for me to be able to see their true beauty. As God has taught me these lessons there has been a process of setting them in my life, transforming me bit by bit. There are still lots of rough diamonds and unfinished settings, but I am starting to see how He is fitting things together.

I hope that as you have read this book that your hunger has been whetted for more of God. God made each of us as individuals, each unique. One thing I love about God is the way that He makes each thing different. I marvel at the many different ways that He thought of to make a leaf, let alone the incredible variety of fish or insects or animals. I believe that the closer we get to God and the more we become like Him the more we will be uniquely ourselves. God doesn't want us to become like each other. He has made us so that we each are uniquely able to reflect different aspects of Him.

As you read my stories, take from them that which blesses you and leave the rest. Ask God how you can use these diamonds in your own life but use them in a way that reflects your own uniqueness, not as a copy of anyone else.

If there are particular diamonds that resonated with you I would encourage you to spend time with God meditating on them, asking Him what else He wants you to know about that topic. Take these lessons and make them your own!

I encourage you to keep trusting God, to keep asking Him to reveal Himself to you more fully. Diamonds are formed through time and pressure. These lessons have come to me over years, and there is still so much for me to learn. Our journey with God is a marathon, not a sprint. It is so easy to become impatient or discouraged. If you feel that way, ask God to remind you of where you have come from, and what He has already formed in you.

If you have journaled as you have read this book it's a great idea to reread the journal from time to time. It is amazing how much we can forget. For me, writing this book has helped me to focus on what God has done and to work on solidifying it in my life. Keep asking God to show you what He is doing in your life and what diamond He is forming. So often it feels as though nothing is happening, but you can be sure that God is at work.

Often it is helpful to consider these sorts of things in community. Are there people you can discuss this with? Ask God to show you a few people you can share with on the journey. At the end of the book are discussion questions that could be used to work through the book with a group.

Know that you are in my prayers. If God has spoken to you through this book, I would love to hear about it. You can contact me on the email diamondsfromtheking@gmail.com or via my website www.bullockc.com

Endnote

Hearing God

As I have shared some of these stories with people, one question that often comes up is how does God communicate? I could write a whole book on this (and lots of books have been written!), but I thought I would share briefly how God speaks to me.

I have never heard God as an audible voice or seen a vision. My hearing tends to be much less spectacular than that. It is often just a quiet knowing, a thought that is not my thought. Often, I will ask God a question, and as I wait on Him, I write down the thoughts that come. Sometimes it is hard to know if it is me or Him as it feels very natural, but often as I look back over what I have written I know that those are not my thoughts. They are not my way of thinking. I always check those thoughts against God's revealed word in the Bible. If they conflict I know that it is not God's voice that I am hearing. But if they line up with God's word, and they resonate with my spirit I believe that God is speaking to me.

Another way that God communicates with me is through pictures in my mind. As I pray I might start to see a picture. It is often fleeting, but if I pay attention and ask God about it He often reveals more to me.

Of course, God speaks to me through the Bible. I have read the Bible all my life, and there are passages I have read countless times. I love it when I am reading the Bible and suddenly a sentence or a phrase leaps out at me, and I am filled with excitement or curiosity. It's like God has used a highlighter to bring my attention to it. Again, my normal response is to talk to God about it, to ask Him to show me more. Sometimes He does, and sometimes He leaves it to sit in my heart for a while.

I also find God speaks to me by showing me patterns in the Bible. Like the chapter on disappointment, where God seemed to highlight different stories in the Bible and how they were similar to one another. Meditating on the big story of the Bible often helps me to hear God better.

Another way that I think God speaks to me is through a 'knowing'. It is hard to explain, but it is a deep sense of knowing something that you didn't know before, which brings a peace in my spirit.

Jesus promised that if we were his sheep that we would hear his voice. (John 10:4). If you are a Christian, then God will be speaking to you. However, hearing His voice can take practice. If this is new to you, I encourage you to ask God to help you to hear Him, and start asking Him questions and wait to hear what He says!

Becoming a Christian

If you have read this book and you don't yet know Jesus, my prayer is that it will help to open your heart to Him. Jesus is always waiting with His arms wide open to welcome people into His family. Becoming a Christian costs nothing and costs everything. When Jesus died on the cross He paid 100% of the price for our sins. We have nothing to pay – all our debt and shame and guilt is taken away if we accept Him. We cannot earn salvation. But becoming a Christian means a change in every part of your life. It means giving up control of your life and making Jesus the Lord of all. Becoming a Christian means changing your priorities and your identity. You become a child of God.

Becoming a Christian is very simple. It just means asking God to forgive you for all the wrong that you have done and choosing to accept Jesus as the Lord of your life. Jesus promises that if we reach out to Him, He will come to us and live with us. He will send the Holy Spirt to teach, comfort and guide us.

If you make this decision, please make sure that you tell a Christian friend about it so that they can journey with you and help you with the next steps. If you don't know any Christians, you could contact a local church. I'm sure they would be thrilled to welcome you! If the first church you try doesn't feel like a good fit, try another. There are lots of options. I'd love to hear from you too! Email me on diamondsfromtheking@gmail.com or via my website www.bullockc.com.

Group Discussion Questions

Notes For The Leader

This is not a traditional Bible study, rather it is a chance for a group to get together and support each other as they work through the material in this book. There is a lot of material covered each week, and it may raise significant issues in people's lives. Don't feel that you have to discuss every question – focus on those that seem most relevant to the group. I have provided a couple of possible activation activities most weeks. Feel free to use them or not, depending on what you feel would be most helpful for participants.

Week 1 – Introduction

Spend some time introducing yourselves to each other. You might like to answer questions like:

> What is your name and living situation?
> How do you spend your time?
> What have been some key highlights of your faith journey?
> Why are you interested in looking at this book?

Group Agreement

This book discusses some quite personal issues. It is important that the group is safe place. To help this, it is a good idea to make a group agreement. As a group, discuss what is important to you to make the group safe for sharing. Record your agreement.

Some areas that you might like to include are: attendance, keeping to time-frames, non-judgmental listening, no advice-giving, giving each person time to share, confidentiality.

Read the Introduction to the book
1. How do you respond to the statement that God doesn't want to destroy anything in our lives? Do you think it is true? Why or why not?
2. Can you identify any lies that you used to believe about God and yourself? What truth has He replaced it with?
3. Can you give an example of something that God has transformed in your life?
4. Is there an area you are longing for God to transform?
5. How does God speak to you?
6. Read aloud the verse at the beginning of the Introduction, changing the *you* to *I*. How does that feel?

Pray for one another

Remind everyone to read Chapters 1-4 and do the reflection questions before next week's meeting.

Week 2 – Who am I? Chapters 1-4

1. What stood out from this week's chapters? Was there anything in particular that you identified with?
2. How did you react to the idea that God's focus is on you, not your sin?
3. Discuss the story of John in Chapter 2. Can you identify ways that you have stayed in the rubbish heap trying to build your own righteousness rather than living in the righteousness given by Christ?
4. What things did God show you would be in your house of righteousness?
5. In the story or the prodigal son, which brother do you most identify with? Why?
6. How would your life be different if you didn't feel you needed to earn God's love? (or do you already believe it?)
7. Where do you believe that God is growing you at the moment?

Activation

Possible activities:

1. On a sheet of paper draw a picture of your house of righteousness. What rooms are in it? What rooms are you using most? Where is God in the house?
2. Imagine that you are one of the sons in the parable of the Prodigal Son (whichever one you identify with). What would you like to say to God? What do you think God wants to say to you?

Pray for one another

Each person chose a lie that they have identified or an area where they would like to grow that has been highlighted by this week's reading. Pray for each other in these areas.

For next week
Read Section 2 – Chapters 5-9

Week 3 – What am I? Chapters 5-9

1. What stood out from this week's chapters? Was there anything in particular that you identified with?
2. How do you feel about your body, and this physical world?
3. How could you use your body to worship God? What works best for you? Would you like to try something new?
4. Is there a creative area you would like to explore?
5. How do you react to the idea of God giving you glory? Did God show you anything about how He is glorifying you?
6. How is God using you as light in your world, or how would you like Him to use you?
7. What is your response to God seeing you as a pearl of great price? Does it change how you see yourself?
8. What verses did you chose to speak over yourself in Chapter 9's reflections?

Activation

Possible activities:
1. Put on some worship music and spend some time worshipping God using your body. You might like to kneel or raise your hands or lie flat on your face (something Moses seems to have done a lot) or dance. It might help to dim the lights and make some space if possible.
2. Close your eyes and ask God to give you a picture of what your light looks like. Imagine going about your day with that light touching each person you meet.

Pray for one another

Each participant shares which identity issue they would like to become more true in their own life – enjoying their body, being given glory by God, being light or being a pearl of great price. Pray for each other in these areas.

For next week
Read Section 3 – Chapters 10-15

Week 4 - Where is God when Life Hurts? Chapters 10-15

1. What stood out from this week's chapters? Was there anything in particular that you identified with?
2. What is a characteristic lie you find yourself believing as a consequence of a childhood wound (Chapter 10)? What impact has that had? What truth has God shown you in response to it?
3. Briefly share a time of suffering from your life.
4. How has God shown Himself faithful to you in the midst of suffering, or as you have reflected on it?
5. Can you share any wisdom with the group in how you have experienced grief or suffering?
6. How do you feel about acknowledging your weakness and God's strength? What is hard for you about that?
7. Do you have a favourite verse that comforts you in hard seasons?

Activation
Possible activities:
1. Imagine yourself sitting on Father God's lap, as a little child. Tell Him about your hurts and see what He does in return.
2. Pick one of the verses shared in question 7. Draw a picture or diagram that represents what it means for you. Try to memorise the verse.

Pray for one another
If anyone is currently in a season of suffering, pray for them, and pray for each other in areas that have been raised by this week's stories.

For next week
Read Section 4 – Chapters 16-19

Week 5 – When God Does the Unexpected. Chapters 16-19

1. What stood out from this week's chapters? Was there anything in particular that you identified with?
2. How have you experienced the Holy Spirit in your life? How do you react to the author's experience?
3. How has God disappointed you? What was your response?
4. Are there any areas of your life where you feel you have lost hope?
5. Did you watch a video of a potter working on a wheel? How did imagining God forming you in that way impact you?
6. What was your reaction to the reflection on Mary's story? Would you describe her as blessed? Does her story change how you see your story?

Activation
Possible activities:
1. Sit with your hands open palm up in your lap. Imagine that your hands are full of the disappointments and hurts you are holding onto in your walk with God. As you feel ready, ask God to take them from your hands and ask Him to show you what He wants to give you in their place.
2. Next Sunday, try visiting to a church that has a more charismatic approach to worship than your regular church. Try not to be judgmental of what you might see. Ask Holy Spirit to reveal Himself to you in a new way, and to show you how he is working.

Pray for one another
Pray for areas of disappointment that people have shared, particularly areas that they have lost hope.

If there is anyone in the group who longs for an experience of Holy Spirit, whatever God choses for that to look like, pray for them.

For next week
Read Section 5 – Chapters 20-24

Week 6 – God in the Everyday Chapters 20-24
1. What stood out from this week's chapters? Was there anything in particular that you identified with?
2. How do spiritual disciplines work for you? Which, if any, do you do? What motivates you?
3. How does God's 'three-in-one'-ness impact your everyday life? Is there a member of the Trinity you would like to get to know better? What things could you do to start that process?
4. What do you rely on fear to do for you? How can you start trusting God for that?
5. Do you have more trouble with letting go of seasons that are passing, or with wishing away the season that you are in? What could you do this week to enjoy the season you are currently in?

Conclusion
How has this study impacted you? What is one thing you will take away? How can you continue to support one another? Pray for each other

www.ingramcontent.com/pod-product-compliance
Lightning Source LLC
Chambersburg PA
CBHW060521100426
42743CB00009B/1396